TENNIS

TENNIS

WARD LOCK

ANNE PANKHURST ·

Series Editor Ian Morrison
Designed by Anita Ruddell
Illustrations by Tony Randell

Text set in 10/11pt Compugraphic Triumvirate by BP Integraphics, Bath, Avon
Printed and bound in Great Britain at The Bath Press, Avon

British Library Cataloguing in Publication Data
Pankhurst, Anne
    Tennis – (Ahead of the game)
    1. Lawn tennis
    I. Title II. Series
    796.342

    ISBN 0–7063–6870–3

Acknowledgements

The author and publishers would like to thank the following for supplying the photographs reproduced in this book:
Colorsport pp 2, 7, 10, 16, 20, 23, 26, 29, 37, 43, 45, 59, 62, 63, 74, 78, 93, 107, 109, 117, 118;
Sporting Pictures (UK) Ltd pp 13, 87, 113;
Allsport pp 114, 123

Frontispiece: Bjorn Borg, centre court, centre stage, as always; his technical brilliance was allied to a level of fitness which has probably never been surpassed by any other tennis player.

CONTENTS

INTRODUCTION

This book is intended to help you develop your tennis skills. You probably understand the elementary tactics, the rules and the fundamentals of hitting the ball for a forehand, backhand, serve and volley – even if you cannot do them as well as you would like. Your aim now is to become a better player and perhaps join a good club and play matches.

This book will try to help you in three ways:

1. It will increase your understanding of tactics and matchplay.

2. It will widen your stroke repertoire and show you how some of the top players play the game.
3. It will advise you on how to get fit to play the game well, and to prevent personal injuries as much as possible.

What a book cannot do is to make all these things happen for you. Only hard work, practice and perhaps some coaching can do that. It takes time, however, so be patient.

Anne Pankhurst

Miloslav Mecir is not amongst the classic serve-and-volley players who have come to dominate tennis today; but his marvellous repertoire of shots and pinpoint accuracy are sometimes enough to beat the best in the world, and are a delight for knowledgeable spectators everywhere.

INTRODUCTION

ONE

CHOOSING TENNIS EQUIPMENT

When choosing tennis equipment you are usually faced with a bewildering array of rackets, shoes and clothes. Even tennis balls come in different colours. In addition, equipment designs change from year to year, and it can be hard to know where to start.

TENNIS · RACKETS

Materials

Tennis rackets are made of a variety of materials. Rackets made of aluminium are the cheapest, followed by composite rackets. These are made of a mixture of fibreglass and graphite, and maybe other materials such as kevlar, boron or ceramic. The most expensive rackets have more graphite and less fibreglass, but may still have a percentage of other materials.

As a simple rule, the more expensive a racket is, the better quality it is likely to

be, but there are other points to consider.

A composite racket is probably easier to play with than an aluminium one because it is more powerful and you do not need to work so hard. However, you may find a very expensive graphite racket stiff and unresponsive. If you are a club player, you would probably be sensible to choose a racket in the middle of the price range – but you ought to have two in case a string breaks in a match.

Shape

The shape of the racket also varies. First the string area will vary from racket to racket and, second, the width of the frame may be wide or narrow. The current models are 'wide-beam' rackets and the frame is thick.

Some rackets have a protective 'bumper' strip on the top of the head, which is a good idea. If you inadvertently hit the ground this strip protects the frame and can be replaced by the stringer. One advantage of the aluminium framed racket is that it will only bend if it hits the ground, whereas frames made of other materials can crack or break.

What size of racket should you choose? A mid-size frame is currently the most popular, but you could have an over-size one. Either of these has an advantage over the old, normal size frame because the 'sweet spot' of the strings is bigger. That means you should have a better chance of hitting the ball hard and well, and more often.

Weight

The weight of the racket is also important. The weight will determine how well and easily you can swing the racket. If it is too heavy then it will make your arm tire quickly. Using a racket that is too light will mean that you tend to lose control of it easily. It should feel comfortable.

Grip size

The grip size should be such that, as you hold the racket, the nail of your index finger and your thumb nail should just overlap. Too small or too large a grip will put a strain on your fore-arm muscles and could lead to tennis elbow. Many players are putting soft, wrap-round grips on their rackets on top of the original grip, which obviously increases the grip size and carries the same dangers as using a racket with too large a grip.

Strings

The next consideration is the strings. Most rackets sold in the British Isles are already strung. It is difficult to know what these strings are made of, and you can only assume that the tension is correct. When you need a re-string you must be sure that the new strings are put in at the right tension and that they are of good quality.

Never replace just one or two broken strings – always have them all replaced. If a string breaks it is a good idea to cut *all* the strings to prevent excessive tension on one side of the frame, and then take your racket to a knowledgeable stringer as soon as possible. You must make sure the stringer knows what sort of player you are so that he will choose a suitable string and the right tension for your style of play. The tension will obviously need to be within the tension range recommended by the manufacturer, and adjusted to suit the string used. Poor stringing and, in particular stringing to a tension above that recommended can easily damage or break the frame. Many players believe that tight strings allow you to hit the ball harder. However, this is not true and you should in fact reduce the tension a little if you want extra power on your strokes.

TENNIS · BALLS

Some tennis clubs still supply tennis balls free to their members or alternatively sell them at a reduced price. However, if you have to buy them in a shop then there is a wide choice.

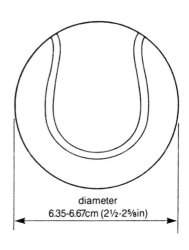

diameter
6.35-6.67cm (2½-2⅝in)

Some are called pressureless balls which means that, in theory, they will stay firm over quite a long period of time. If you only need to use your own tennis balls infrequently, then these can be a good buy. Most tennis balls, though, are sold in sealed cans and will lose their pressure fairly quickly once the can is unsealed. They will gradually lose their bounce over a period of several months. (Until the container is unsealed they should keep indefinitely.)

Some tennis balls have 'long-lasting' cloth and it is claimed that they last longer on very abrasive courts. Once the cloth starts to wear out the ball becomes lighter and behaves differently. It is. therefore, a good idea to make sure all the balls you are playing with are of the same type and age, and that they are not becoming bald. Sometimes it is possible to buy used tournament balls or 'seconds' much cheaper than new tennis balls. Seconds are all right for practice as long as their fault is in the cloth, and not in the bounce.

SHOES

This is another item of tennis equipment where it is easy to be confused by the range available.

In the case of shoes, the most expensive are not necessarily the best, and there is no point in paying simply for a name. The important thing when buying tennis shoes is that they should fit and be comfortable. When you try them on, wear the same sort of socks that you play in. Be sure that the heel tab is soft and will not cause pressure on your Achilles tendon. Leather shoes will be more comfortable and cooler than canvas or nylon ones. The sole should not be heavily 'ribbed' as some jogging shoes are. If you play on a variety of surfaces then you should consider buying different pairs to suit each surface. Generally speaking the more grip the court has, the less grip you need on the sole of your shoes.

CLOTHING

Many tennis clubs still prefer predominantly white clothing, so, to be on the safe side, buy clothing along those lines. Again, sports goods shops stock a wide range of clothing, at an equally wide range of prices.

You obviously need comfortable socks, a tennis shirt, shorts (or skirt), and a pullover. A tracksuit is very useful and allows you to warm up comfortably, as well as keeping you warm after a game. It is also a good idea to have a bag of some description to take on court, containing a towel, first aid kit, spare racket and spare clothing.

The indomitable Billie Jean King's final appearance at Wimbledon in 1983; at times throughout her extraordinary long career, it seemed that she beat younger and perhaps more gifted players through sheer heart.

TWO

THE
BASICS
REVISED

Although this book is for people already familiar with the basics of tennis, there are two good reasons for looking at them again. The first is to refresh your memory, but the second is more important. You need a sound basis of knowledge on which to build new ideas, information and advice. Obviously if your understanding of the basic principles is confused or incorrect, then it will be very difficult for you to make good, consistent progress.

BASIC · GRIPS

By now as an improving player, you will have settled on a comfortable grip for all your strokes. However, it is possible either that your grips are not quite correct, or that you need to modify them if you want to extend your range of strokes.

The three **forehand grips** are the eastern, the semi-western (or western) and the continental. Each of these has its own advantages. As you improve you will recognise the different grips used by your opponents and will learn the best tactics to use against them.

The **backhand grip** will be either single- or two-handed, or may start off two-handed until just after you have hit the ball, when you release your supporting hand.

Your **service grip** will probably have been an Eastern forehand grip when you started playing tennis and should, as you improve, be changed to a continental grip. This grip, sometimes called the Chopper grip, will give you more speed off the racket head, so you hit the ball harder. It will also make it possible to learn a spin serve.

The basic **volley grip** changes from a forehand to a backhand, depending on which side you are volleying. Again, once your are no longer a beginner you will

The semi-western forehand as shown by Ivan Lendl.

With a semi-western grip, the arm is slightly bent and the ball is hit at a higher point (when possible) than is the case with the eastern or continental grips. The body may turn more to the side.

need to change to a continental grip so that you can play either the forehand or backhand volley without changing your grip. This will be a particular advantage when the ball is travelling very quickly and is close to the net.

BASIC · STROKES

If you want to play a better game, then sound stroke production is essential. It is much easier to concentrate on winning your game if you are not worrying about hitting your backhand or moving in to volley.

Racket control

The vital thing to remember about hitting a tennis ball is to adapt your stroke according to the type of shot you want to make. The groundstrokes, the forehand and the backhand, need to propel a relatively slow-moving ball over quite a long distance. To achieve this, you must **swing** your racket at the ball to ensure enough speed in the racket-head at the moment of impact.

As well as swinging the racket, you must try to get the **path** of the racket swing effective. The racket should be taken back early and brought from just below the height of the ball with the racket face slightly open, to hit the ball up and over the net. The racket head should finish in front of you. With the semi-

THE · BASICS · REVISED

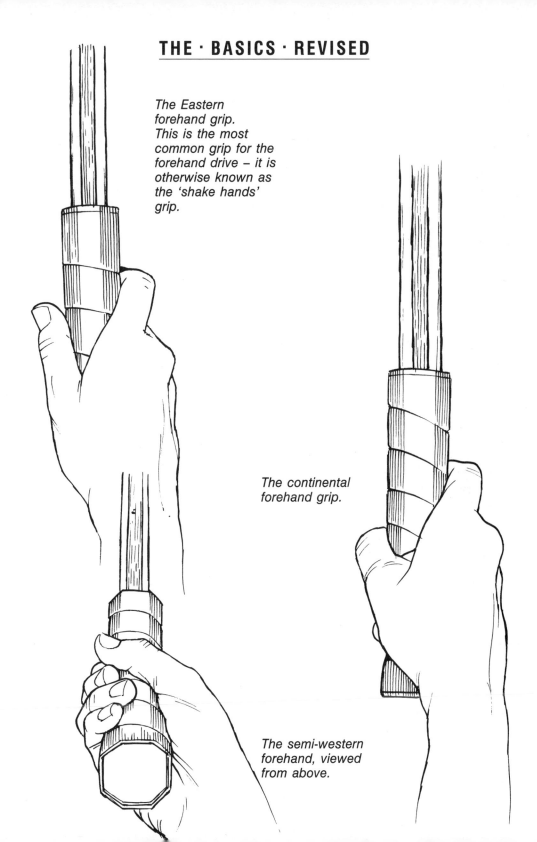

The Eastern forehand grip. This is the most common grip for the forehand drive – it is otherwise known as the 'shake hands' grip.

The continental forehand grip.

The semi-western forehand, viewed from above.

THE · BASICS · REVISED

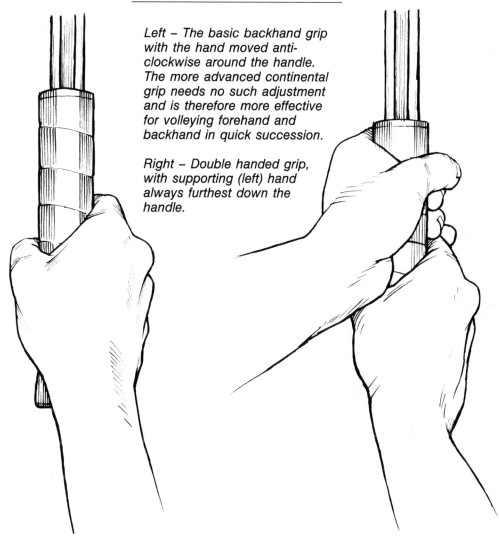

*Left – The basic backhand grip
with the hand moved anti-
clockwise around the handle.
The more advanced continental
grip needs no such adjustment
and is therefore more effective
for volleying forehand and
backhand in quick succession.*

*Right – Double handed grip,
with supporting (left) hand
always furthest down the
handle.*

western grip the ball will be struck at a
higher point and consequently the racket
face needs to be more closed to the ball.
   In the service you must also hit the ball
quite a distance, starting with it virtually
stationary. This needs even more power,

so you must **throw** your racket head at
the ball. The volley is rather different. It is
played close to the net and consequently
the ball has a relatively short distance to
travel into your opponent's court. The ball
is still moving quite fast when it gets to
you, so you should **punch** it back down
across the net. If you swing at it you will
probably miss it!

Spain's Arantxa Sanchez has recently
made a great impact on the women's
circuit. Here she shows how to play the
two-handed backhand.

TENNIS

Ball contact point X for the backhand (for the right-hander).

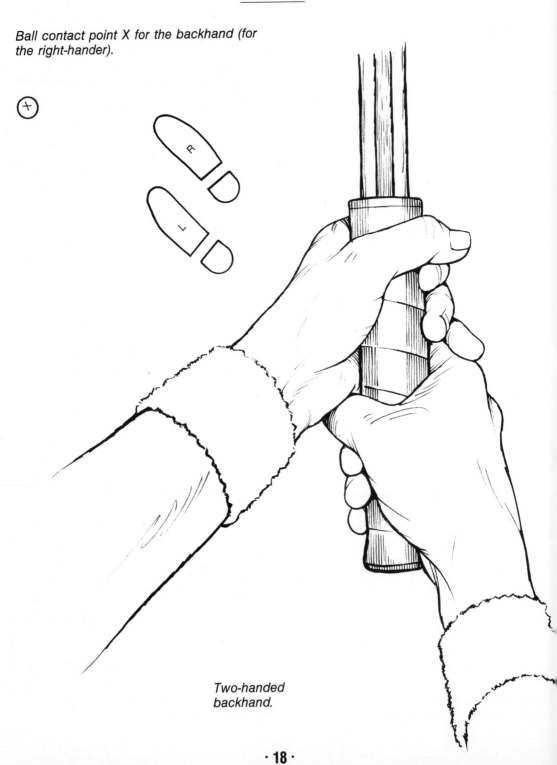

Two-handed backhand.

Position of the ball

In addition to the correct use of the racket head a second important factor is the position of the ball in relation to you. On the groundstrokes the ball needs to be hit when it is a comfortable distance from you. If you hold the racket on the forehand with either the Eastern or Continental grip then your arm will be almost straight and the ball will be hit from a point somewhere between your knee and waist. If you have a Semi-Western grip then your arm will be slightly bent and you will find it more comfortable to hit the ball at a higher point.

As well as being at the right height, the ball needs to be in such a position that the racket has enough room and distance to swing. The player with an Eastern forehand will want to hit the ball slightly in front of his front foot. The player who uses the Continental grip on the forehand is more comfortable hitting the ball slightly further back, while someone using the Semi-Western grip may not turn sideways very much, but will still hit the ball slightly in front.

On the backhand, whether single-handed or two-handed, you must turn and try to hit the ball in line with your front foot, so that again the racket has room and distance to swing.

Distance to side of body

Height of ball

*Eastern or continental grip
– distance to side of body.*

*Eastern or continental grip
– height of ball.*

Semi-western grip – distance to side of body.

Semi-western grip – height of ball.

On the service the racket head is thrown at the ball. You should try to place the ball just on your racket side, and high enough for your arm and racket to be at full stretch, with the racket head slightly ahead of your front foot at the moment of impact. Throw the ball up so that, if you did not hit it, it would land just inside the baseline.

Mats Wilander shows how to play the low ball with a two-handed backhand.

When volleying, your racket should punch the ball, which must still be in the right place in relation to you. Since you hit the ball before it has bounced, the height at which you have to hit it is decided by your opponent. But you *can* position yourself so that the ball is on your racket side and slightly in front of you, to give yourself the best chance of hitting it well. The racket must come from an up start position so that you volley the ball down into your opponent's court.

Ball contact point X for the right-handed player adopting the eastern forehand grip.

Ball contact position X for the right-handed player adopting the semi-western forehand grip.

Ball contact point X for the right-handed player adopting the continental forehand grip.

BASIC · PRINCIPLES

In addition to hitting the ball correctly and being in the right position there are five general principles of sound stroke production:

1. Watch the ball.
2. Have good footwork.
3. Have good balance.
4. Control the racket *head* .
5. Control the racket *face* .

If your stroke is sound and effective, then you are obeying all five of these rules. If, however, something is going wrong, you are failing to observe one (or more!) of them.

Jana Novotna shows the key points of a good backhand.

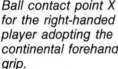

TENNIS

Throw ball up to racket side – but not too much.

Ball at correct height, with arm at full stretch.

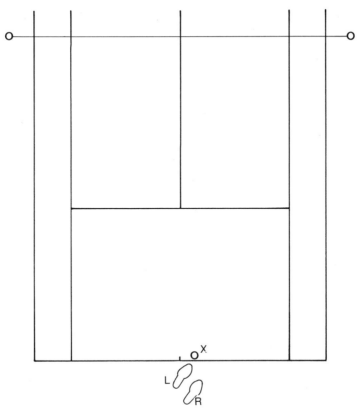

At service, the contact point of the ball X should be slightly in front of the left foot.

Watching the ball

All tennis players are sure they do this, but the important point is *when* they start to watch it. As your tennis skills develop so the ball travels faster and perhaps has spin on it. This means that you must watch the ball very closely from the moment your opponent hits it. You must also try to pick up clues about what the ball is going to do from the way in which he strikes it. Perhaps the racket head starts very low and finishes quite high as he hits his forehand. This indicates a top-spin forehand. Perhaps he throws the ball quite far out to the side on a serve, telling you that a slice service is coming.

Watching the ball at all times will give you valuable information and help you to judge its movement more effectively.

Good footwork

The speed and spin on the ball will cause the bounce to vary. It is vital that both your movement around the court and your footwork positioning as you hit the ball, are quick. Generally speaking, several small steps are better than one large one. Keep your feet underneath you if you possibly can so that you can change direction quickly. It is much more difficult to do this, or to start moving in the first place, if your feet are far apart.

Good balance

This is an essential part of good shot making. If your body is balanced as you strike the ball then you stand a better chance of hitting it well. Again, as you improve, it becomes more difficult to get your feet in the right position because of the faster pace of the returned ball, and keeping your body balanced becomes all the more important.

Control of the racket head

When you play tennis well, or watch good players, you have the feeling that the racket is completely under control. The player knows exactly where it is and what it is doing. It doesn't matter whether he is playing a groundstroke, volley or serve, the good player always uses the racket correctly. The novice player, on the other hand, often 'snatches' at the volley or 'pushes' his serve. As you improve, the number of occasions when the stroke feels right will increase. This is because you have controlled the racket throughout the swing, throw or punch. The correct grip will help considerably.

Control of the racket face

As you swing, throw, or punch the stroke, not only should the racket be under your control but the face (the strings) must hit the ball at exactly the right angle. To ensure this your wrist must control the racket face throughout the stroke. If you lose control, the ball is likely to go too high over the net, or straight into it.

Stefan Edberg of Sweden is one of the world's leading servers and here he demonstrates his technique to the fullest.

BASIC · TACTICS

As you meet better players, your opponents have more ideas for outwitting you, so you need more ideas too. With a combination of more tactics and a greater range of strokes, you can vary your returns and improve your ability to return difficult strokes from your opponent.

Keeping the ball in play

The only fundamental aim in tennis is to get the ball over the net into the court one more time than your opponent. Sometimes it is easy to forget this, especially if you are trying hard to improve one small part of a stroke. But there is no point in having perfect style if you cannot get the ball over the net consistently. Unless you can do this, you cannot hope to win enough points to win matches. You cannot work on the principle that your opponent will make mistakes and so let you win. You have to make him play the ball.

TENNIS

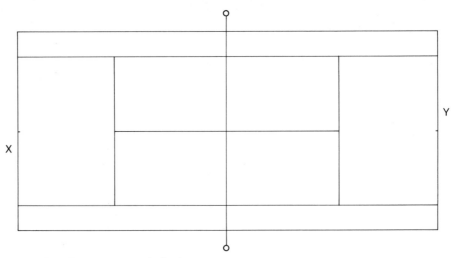

Starting a game of singles
X – Server's position in a game of singles
Y – Receiver's position in a game of singles
There are several basic reasons for the server to play from this
position; first it gives him the best opportunity to attack the
backhand of a (right-handed) opponent. If the server stands
too far to the right, he more or less cuts out this possibility;
and he is also out of position for any return to his left.

Making your opponent run

The next thing is to try to make it difficult for your opponent to get the ball back into your court. Tactically, if you make your opponent run then he will not have time to think or settle down, and so cannot build up his timing, or confidence. Use all the court. Hit the ball wide on some occasions, and straight at him as a variation at other times. Hit the ball short or deep, sometimes hard and sometimes quite softly, and also try to vary whether you hit it close to the net and high in the air. In other words, 'mix up' your returns so as to keep your opponent guessing, and at the same time make him a little anxious!

Positioning yourself

The problem is that your opponent will be using the same tactics on you, so you need a way to reduce their effects. The best strategy for this is to try to get a good position on the court. As soon as you have hit the ball you must move into position to deal with the return. Many beginners hit the ball and stand watching to see where it goes, which means that they are never ready for the return.

If you are playing singles you must be in the right position at the start of the game and during the rally. The diagrams show you where to start, depending on whether you are the server or receiver. As soon as you have served, or returned the

Argentina's Gabriela Sabatini shows the 'ready' position.

TENNIS

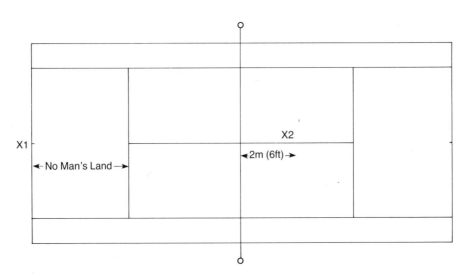

Players' positions during a rally in singles
X1 = Baseline rallying position in singles
X2 = Volleying position in singles

ball if you are the receiver, then you must move either to the baseline position or volleying position.

If you are rallying from the back of the court, go to the **baseline position** and try to stay back around the middle of the baseline between shots if you can. Then you only have half the court to cover to get to a return. If the ball drops short of the baseline you can always run forwards. It is very difficult to reach a shot which goes behind you. If a shot does that, then you are too far inside the baseline in what is called 'no man's land'.

Sometimes during a rally your opponent will return the ball short, in other words, between the net and the service line. You will then have the opportunity to move forward to the **volleying position**. Return the ball deep to give yourself more time to get to the net. The volleying position is about 2–3m (6–8ft) back from the net.

If you are playing doubles you take up a slightly different position at the start of the game. The server should move towards the side line (which is further away than for singles because the

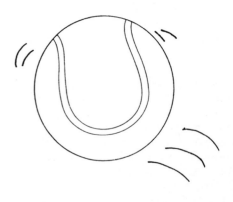

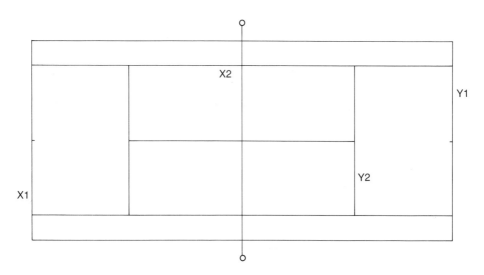

Starting a game of doubles
X1 = Server's position
X2 = Server's partner
Y1 = Receiver
Y2 = Receiver's partner

tramlines are in use) so that he can cover his half of the court. The receiver is in a similar position to that in singles, so that he can cover serves to either the forehand or backhand. The server's partner should take up a volleying position near the net so that he can block off his sideline, but in such a position that he will not get hit by the ball from the serve. The receiver's partner should stand on his service line so that he can immediately move forwards, or backwards, depending on his partner's return.

Once the serve and return of serve are completed it is vital that you and your partner get level with each other, either on the baseline or up at the net. If you don't, you will give the opposition a perfect opportunity to hit into the gaps between you. We will talk about that further in Chapter Four which deals with more advanced tactics.

Being ready for the ball

As well as being in the right place on the court you need to be ready to hit the ball. This means that your racket needs to be ready to move quickly to either side and your body should be ready to move in any direction. Your knees should be bent, your feet about shoulder width apart and your body should feel ready. Look at the picture of Gabriela Sabatini on page 29 receiving service – she is totally ready for action. Even if you are the server, it is still important to adopt the correct position.

It is actually quite difficult to be scientific about the correct stance for receiving service; if you watch the professionals you will see that some crouch lower than others, some have their feet very wide apart, and that players hold their rackets in different positions. A great deal of this crouching, racket swinging etc. is little more than psychological.

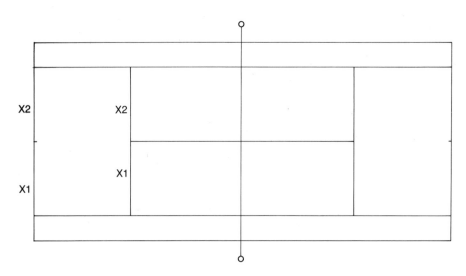

*Correct positions during a rally in doubles
Either X1–X1 or X2–X2 is correct.*

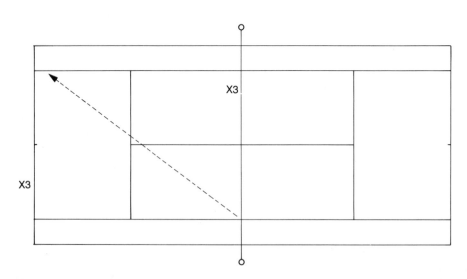

*Incorrect position during a rally in doubles
X3–X3 is incorrect because it leaves the
diagonal gap for the opposition to play in
to. (See page 77).*

THREE

IMPROVING YOUR

TECHNIQUE

At the moment, as a developing player, you know the basic groundstrokes, and can hit a reasonable forehand and backhand. You know how to serve, and can hit a medium-pace ball into court. You have mastered basic volleying, and can sometimes win the point with a good volley. At this stage it would be helpful, and would allow you more options in a game, if you were able to vary your existing strokes and add some new ones to your repertoire. The main technique for varying your strokes is to master the art of spinning the ball.

THE · PRINCIPLES · OF
THE · SPIN

The basic strokes of the game ensure that the ball is hit fairly flat (without spin) and travels on a recognisable flight path. For example, the flat forehand travels across the court, usually reaching its highest point over the net. Its bounce is predictable and the receiver can judge, with experience, where it is going to land.

The flat service has the same predictable bounce, and it has to land in a much smaller area, making it easy for the receiver to place himself in the best position to return it.

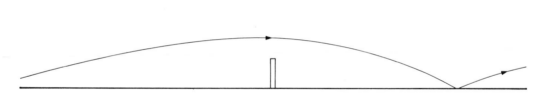

The flight path of the flat forehand.

TENNIS

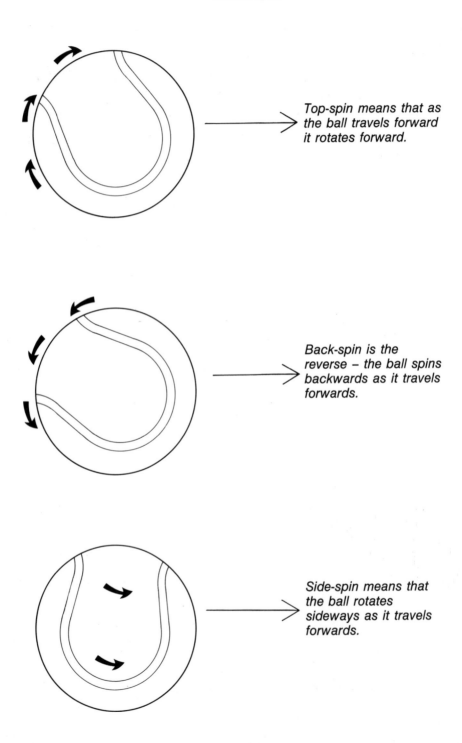

Top-spin means that as the ball travels forward it rotates forward.

Back-spin is the reverse – the ball spins backwards as it travels forwards.

Side-spin means that the ball rotates sideways as it travels forwards.

IMPROVING · YOUR · TECHNIQUE

If you use spin, however, the flight and bounce of the ball become less predictable, and your opponent will find life more difficult.

There are essentially three types of spin:

1. Top-spin, when the ball rotates forwards in the direction it is travelling.
2. Back-spin (called slice on the groundstrokes), when the ball spins backwards.
3. Side-spin (called slice on the serve), when the ball rotates sideways.

The use of these is an essential part of the development of your technique as a tennis player.

Flight path

In addition to rotating it, the spin will cause the ball to follow a different flight path. The top-spin ball will travel higher over the net but then drop more quickly, so it does not travel as far on your opponent's side of the net as it does on yours. You can see already that here is an advantage for you. Your opponent is expecting the ball to travel towards him, but it falls short into the court. The fact that it is higher over the net should give him a clue, but perhaps not in time.

The back-spin ball travels longer and flatter than the other drives. This actually makes it a little more difficult for you to judge the length, so you have to be careful not to hit the ball out of court. Nevertheless, played correctly, it is an effective stroke.

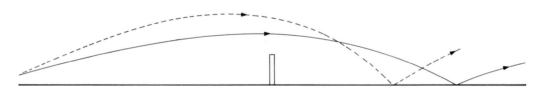

The flight path of the top-spin forehand, shown by the broken line. The flight path of the flat forehand is shown by the unbroken line.

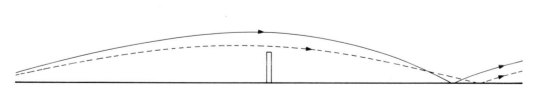

The effect of the flight path of the forehand played with back-spin is shown by the broken line. The unbroken line is the flight path of the normal flat forehand.

TENNIS

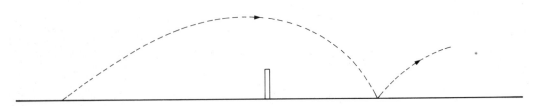

The bounce of a ball hit with top-spin.

The bounce of a ball when hit with back-spin.

Side-spin will again keep the ball low but will also make it move across the court, so that your opponent will find the ball has moved unexpectedly in both length and width. Side-spin is frequently combined with back-spin on groundstrokes. You do this by moving the racket across your body as you swing it forwards.

Bounce

Even if your opponent has judged the flight path of the spinning ball correctly he still has to deal with a difficult bounce. The top-spin ball bounces and kicks up high very quickly, making it very difficult to hit, as your opponent will get pushed back into the stop netting if he waits for it to fall.

The back-spin ball, on the other hand, bounces low but stands straight up. Your opponent is used to the ball coming through to him so has to adjust quickly when he finds it further in front of him than he expected.

The bounce of a ball with side-spin.

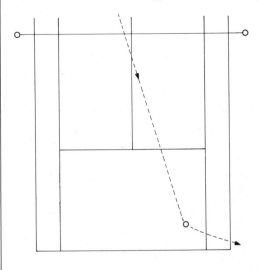

Superbly athletic top-spin serve by the Swede, Jonas Svensson

1

2

The side-spin ball also bounces low, but then swings out away from the point at which it strikes the ground, making it very difficult to play.

Keeping the ball in court

As well as outwitting your opponent by varying the flight and bounce of the ball, the spin has another advantage. It gives you a greater chance of keeping the ball in the court, whilst being able to hit it hard. Top-spin, in particular, keeps the ball in, and is especially useful for a second service. Using slice can often give you time to get to the net to volley, or it can keep the ball low to stop your opponent volleying.

4

Executing a forehand with top-spin. The racket head at the start of the stroke is below the ball.

HOW · TO · PLAY · SPIN

Groundstrokes

To impart spin to a ball on the groundstrokes you need to change the path of the racket swing from your normal fairly flat hit.

For top-spin, the racket head needs to start below the height of the ball. The strings are brushed quickly up and over the ball, *closing* the racket face on the way, and with the racket finishing higher than before. This means that the ball will leave your racket, spinning forwards as it moves and travelling higher over the net than it would with your basic drive.

For back-spin the opposite applies. The racket head will start above the ball, finishing lower than before, and the racket

FOREHAND · DRIVE-SLICE

Executing a forehand with a slice. As your skills improve, you will begin instinctively to anticipate spin when receiving, according to the racket head swing path of your opponent.

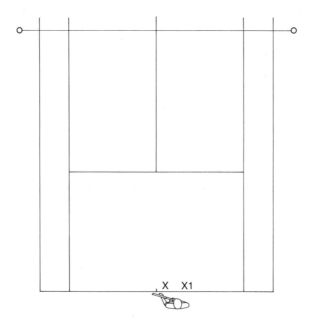

X indicates the point where the ball would land if you threw it up for a flat serve but did not hit it.
X1 is where it would land if you were serving with slice.

face will be open as it strokes the back and slightly underneath the ball. This ensures that the ball spins backwards as it leaves the racket and travels low over the net.

For side-spin, the racket face needs to be brought across the ball by starting with the racket out away from the body and swinging it in towards the body. The strings will therefore brush *across* the ball, giving it side-spin as it travels forwards.

Service

To give spin to your serve you need to change both the placement of the ball and the path of the racket. As you improve your service variations, you will find it possible to place the ball in a similar position for all your serves and so make it more difficult for your opponent to work out what sort of serve you are about to hit. However, at the learning stage it is essential to change the placement of the ball.

The **slice-serve** is quite easy to learn but needs hard work to make it effective. The ball should be placed further away towards the outside of the court than for

Note the high starting position of the racket head as Boris Becker slices a backhand to approach the net.

TENNIS

the flat serve, but it should still be thrown up slightly in front of you. The diagram shows where it would bounce if you didn't hit it – still inside the baseline, but further out towards the side of the court.

The path of the racket throw is then round the outside of the ball, finishing on the opposite side of your body. Obviously because the ball is slightly further away from you, you will not be able to hit it at such a high point, but you should still try to hit it at full stretch.

As the ball leaves the racket it will move to the left (from a right-hander) and as it bounces, move out towards the side line in the right court. This will complicate matters for your opponent who has to judge the different flight and then the

different bounce of the ball.

There is one other point to remember with the slice serve and that is that, because the ball swerves as it travels, it may be necessary to adjust your aim slightly in order to get the ball to land in the service court.

The **top-spin serve** is quite difficult to learn, but is a very effective second serve. It has a very different action from either of the other two serves.

The placement of the ball is now actually behind you — if you think about it, that is the only way in which you could hit top-spin! The ball should be thrown up so that, if you did not hit it, it would run down your back, landing behind both you and the baseline.

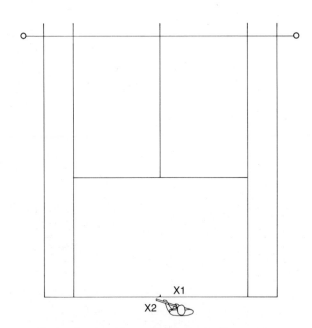

X1 is the position where the ball would land if using a flat service and X2 is its position for the top-spin serve.

The top-spin serve. A superb shot expertly
executed by one of its masters, Stefan Edberg.

SERVICE–SLICE

Executing a service with slice. The racket head makes contact with the 'outside' of the ball – ie the side furthest from the body – and crosses the body to impart spin.

TENNIS

SERVICE-TOPSPIN

Executing a service with top-spin. One of the hardest shots to master; the key to success is the vigorous throw of the racket head up and over the ball before it is thrown outwards towards the side-line.

The path of the racket throw is different from the standard 'backscratch' position. The racket is thrown up and over the ball with a very vigorous motion. From that position it is thrown out towards the side-line and will finish on the side where it began. This is the way to practise it at the learning stage. As the action becomes more refined you will find that you can finish the service in the normal follow-through position. It helps to achieve the top-spin serve if you bend your knees as the racket begins its upwards movement.

This vigorous upwards brush of the strings on the ball, make it initially fly upwards and high over the net, but it then drops suddenly. As the ball bounces it kicks up and may also swerve slightly (to the opposite side from the slice serve) as it lands.

Volleys

There will be occasions, especially if you have to volley from below the height of the net, when you back-spin your shot slightly, simply to get it up and over the net. But, generally speaking, if you have the opportunity to volley, then the whole idea is to put the ball away into your opponent's court quickly and effectively so

that he cannot get it back. Using spin of any sort slows the ball slightly and so gives him a greater chance of dealing with a volley. This is why spin is normally only applied to the groundstrokes and service.

DEVELOPING · NEW · STROKES

As you improve you will find that a greater repertoire of strokes will be an advantage, especially against an opponent who is trying all the time to outwit you.

If, for example, he is a good volleyer, it will be quite difficult to get the ball past him, even if you do use spin to keep the ball low. If you could lob well over his head, you would drive him back from the net to the baseline, and perhaps make him nervous of coming quite so close next time.

If your opponent is an excellent baseline rallyer who gets every ball back, and just waits for you to make a mistake, then a short, soft shot played just over the net will be a great weapon. A wide range of strokes is thus not only a great asset to any prospective club player, it is really as essential. All the strokes in this section are based on the basic strokes, and nearly all

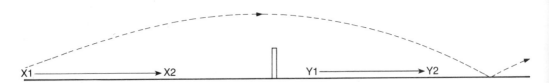

The attacking lob. After playing the lob, X1 is ready to move to X2 in order to attack the net. Y1 will have to retreat to Y2 in order to retrieve the ball.

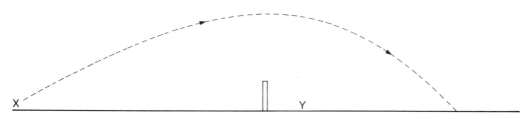

The defensive lob – note the difference in trajectory of the ball.

of them can be varied by using spin. They can be divided up neatly as follows:

1. Those based on groundstrokes: the lob and drop shot.
2. Those based on serves: the smash.
3. Those based on volleys: the stop. volley, drive volley and lob volley.

The flat lob

Essentially the lob is a shot in which the ball is hit high up into the air, over the net, to land just inside your opponent's baseline. It can be used as an attacking shot, to drive your opponent back from the net, and to allow you to take up the net position. Alternatively it can be used defensively, when you hit the ball high in the air to give yourself time to get back into court.

The first thing you will notice from the diagrams is that the attacking lob has a lower flight path (closer to the net) than the defensive one. There is a reason for this. Obviously, you need to hit the attacking lob just high enough to avoid your opponent reaching it with his racket outstretched. But you also want the advantage of speed so that the ball will land before he has time to run back and hit it. The defensive lob, on the other hand, is needed to give you time, and so

needs to be high enough to let you get back and recover.

When you learn to lob remember that it is very similar to your forehand and backhand groundstrokes. The ball should be in the right position in relation to you and the racket should be taken back early and swung forward to hit the ball.

The difference is that, as you swing it forwards, you must open the face of the racket so that the strings face upwards. The ball will then leave the strings going in an upward direction, and high over the net. The racket head then follows the flight of the ball, so it will finish in a much higher position than it does for your basic groundstrokes.

This is important because if you don't finish with the racket head high and in front of you then you are likely to lean backwards as you hit the ball. The lob will then land short in your opponent's court and give him the opportunity to smash it back at you.

Try to disguise the lob as long as possible. You don't want your opponent to receive an early warning and start to move back, so try to make your lob as much like your basic groundstroke as possible, and leave the opening of the racket face to the last minute.

LOB - SIDE · VIEW

The lob, side view. The follow-through of the racket is important. If you do not follow-through you will tend to lean back in the stroke and drop the ball short.

The top-spin lob

The problem with the flat lob is that it is very difficult to make it land just inside your opponent's baseline. Your margin of error is very small. If you put top-spin on the shot then not only are the flight path and the bounce changed so as to become more difficult for your opponent, but you will also be better able to keep the ball in court. As with the basic lob, it is important to have the ball in the right position, to take back your racket early, and to disguise your intentions as long as possible.

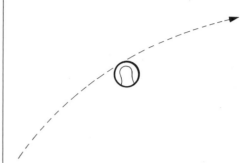

The path of the racket on the forward swing for the top-spin lob.

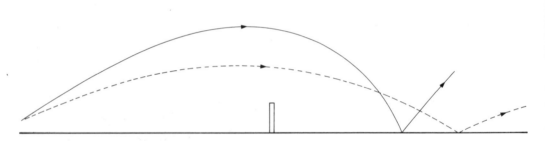

The effect of top-spin when applied to the lob is shown by the unbroken line. The broken line shows the normal flat, attacking lob.

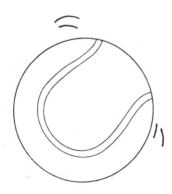

The athletic and graceful Claudia Kohde-Kilsch executes a forehand drive. The six-foot West German was her country's leading player before the arrival of the phenomenal Steffi Graf.

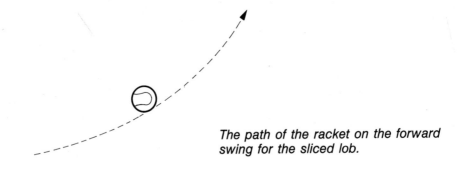

The path of the racket on the forward swing for the sliced lob.

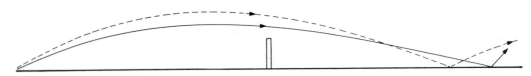

The flight path of the lob played with slice is shown by the unbroken line. The broken line represents the flight path of the lob played without slice.

The flight path of the drop shot.

To hit a lob with top-spin it may help to change your grip to a semi-western on the forehand side (see page 14), even if you don't use one for your basic forehand.

The difference between the flat lob and the top-spin one lies in the forward swing of the racket. It starts below the ball when you hit it and, just like top-spin groundstrokes, brushes up and over the back of the ball with a strong wrist action. The racket head will finish high in front of you, but with the strings facing the ground.

The ball should then leave your racket travelling upwards and go high over your opponent's head. However, the flight path will be different from the ordinary lob and the ball will drop quickly near your opponent's baseline and then 'kick' up high. This means that, even if he does manage to chase the lob, he still has to deal with an awkward bounce and with a ball which drops more quickly than he expected.

The slice lob

Slicing the lob has the same virtues as top-spinning it, but it has the disadvantage of travelling a longer distance, so it needs greater control. The ball will 'hang' in the air, and so the slice lob should be used as a defensive shot giving you time to recover.

The slice lob does not need a change of grip, but it is a difficult shot for a player with a Semi-Western grip. Just like the sliced groundstroke, the racket head must start *above* the ball when you hit it, and the strings hit under the ball. The racket face will be open. Keep your wrist firm and then finish with the racket high in front of you with the strings facing upwards.

The drop shot

The drop shot is a 'surprise' shot – used to change the situation and to break up your opponent's rhythm when he is at the back of the court. The ball is hit so that it drops just over the net and then bounces up. It may even bounce back towards the net so that it is extremely difficult for your opponent to reach. If he manages to scramble and hit it, his return should make an easy possible for you.

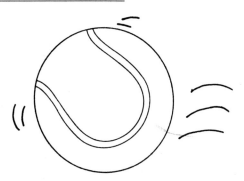

When you learn to play the drop shot, you must apply three of the principles of the lob:

1. The ball should be in the right place in relation to you.
2. The racket should be taken back early.
3. The shot should be disguised as long as possible, to surprise your opponent.

As you bring your racket forward, the strings should be brought down under the ball. Then, to stop as much forward movement as possible, bring the racket up round the front of the ball. The path of the racket head is therefore like a shallow 'U' and the action is rather like turning a large key in a lock. The vital point is that you must take the speed off the ball so that it will just cross the net and land very close to it on your opponent's side of the court.

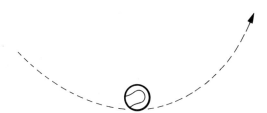

The path of the racket when playing the drop shot.

If you play the ball from too far back on your side of the net then your opponent has plenty of time to see it coming, so it is best to play it from the service line. Of course, the top players hit drop shots from further back than this, but as a club player, learn how to do the shot first and how to keep the ball low in perfect disguise, before you get too ambitious. It is a very different shot from all the others you have learnt so far, because it involves taking the speed off the ball rather than hitting it hard.

The basic smash

The smash is a stroke which is very much like a service action. The ball is hit high above your head and driven hard down into your opponent's court, in the hope that he won't be able to hit it back. The opportunity to smash should be seen as a chance to win the point. Most smashes are hit as the answer to a bad lob, when the ball looks destined to land around the service line instead of the baseline. Obviously, if you are tall and if you have the ability to jump well, you will have an advantage when it comes to the smash.

The action of the smash differs from the serve in three ways:

1. The ball has been put up in the air by your opponent and so you have to get yourself in the right place underneath.
2. You are likely to have to run back in order to get into the right place.
3. Your backswing can be cut short, and the racket can go straight to the 'backscratch' position, if you prefer.

A typical occasion on which you might use a smash is if you are in the volleying position at the net and your opponent sends up a lob. First of all you need to move back and sideways with short sideways steps, *keeping your eye on the ball all the time*. As you move, your racket should be taken back to the 'backscratch' position and your other arm raised in front of you in order to balance your racket arm and body. This is important, and is similar to the way the arm that places the ball in the air acts as a counterbalance to your racket arm, when you serve. Get yourself under the ball, still watching it carefully. It will be dropping towards you, but you must then *throw* your racket, just as you do on the serve, so that you hit it when your arm is at full stretch and the ball is just in front of you on the racket side.

Aim to hit the ball deep into your opponent's court or angle it out towards the sidelines so that in either event he is struggling to hit it back.

John McEnroe completes a smash. Note his position on court.

SMASH – SIDE · VIEW

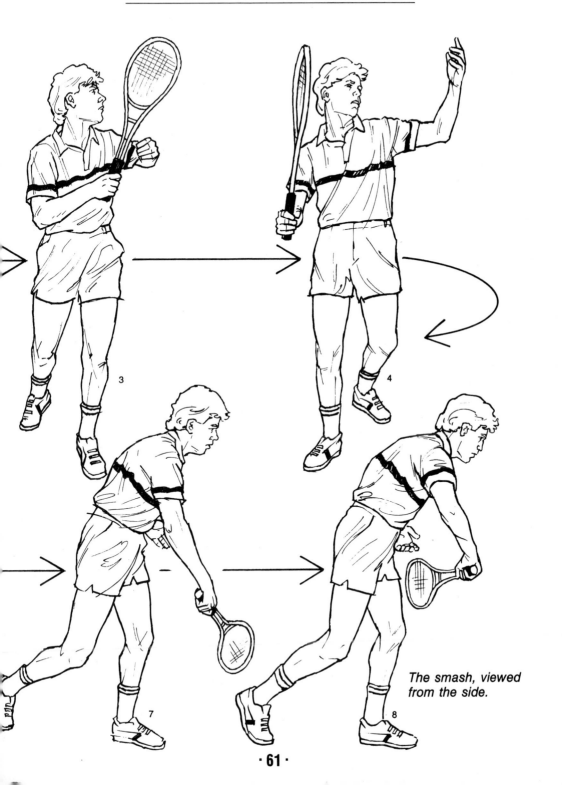

The smash, viewed from the side.

TENNIS

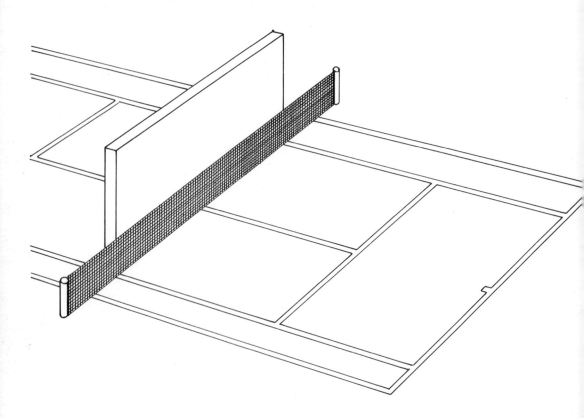

In doubles, volleying is more common than in singles matches.

After serving, the server should move up to the net to volley the service return; the simplest way of thinking about this is to imagine you and your partner as forming an inpenetrable brick wall close into the net.

Is Zina Garrison smashing here or serving? Without reference to the base line, it's impossible to tell. Once you have positioned yourself, the action of the smash is similar to that of the service, with the exception that the backswing can be curtailed when smashing.

TENNIS

The top-spin smash

Just as it is possible to vary your basic serve so you can add spin to the smash.

The top-spin smash is a useful shot. Many lobs will be hit over your backhand, in order to make it more difficult for you to hit them back. But this also means that the ball is dropping into a good position for you to hit it with top-spin, by throwing your racket head up and over the ball. The action is exactly the same as for your top-spin serve. The spin produces a difficult bounce for your opponent to deal with – assuming he actually gets to the ball.

The slice smash

This is another useful shot. Play it exactly as you do the slice serve (page 42) by keeping the ball on your racket side and bringing your racket strings around the outside of the ball. Like the slice serve the slice smash swerves and bounces to the left (from a right-hander), and your opponent will have to deal with a ball which is moving away quickly. This is a good smash to use if you want to hit the ball away at an angle.

The stop volley

The stop (or drop) volley is just what it says. The ball is dropped just over the net so that your opponent has to scramble to get to it. A good stop volley should win the point outright because it is a surprise shot. Your opponent is expecting a hard volley and instead gets a stop volley which 'dies' just over the net.

This is an instance, like the drop shot, where you are aiming to take all the speed off the ball. It is what is called a 'touch shot'. The principles to remember are:

1. Play it off a ball which comes to you either at net height or below.
2. Disguise the shot as much as possible.
3. Follow the principles of good volleying – use neither backswing nor follow through, play the shot with a firm wrist but then open the racket face to come underneath the ball. This will give the ball back-spin. However, at the same time you must take the speed off the ball so that it just drops over the net and either 'dies' or bounces back into the net.
4. If you bend your knees you will find it much easier to play the shot well.

The stop volley.

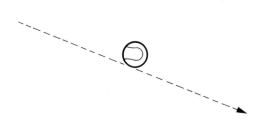

The path of the racket when playing the drive volley.

Clearly, even if your opponent does reach the ball his return is likely to be weak and you ought to win the point off his return. Surprise is vital and so it is best not to play this shot too often. Like all touch shots, it needs practice.

The drive volley

Sometimes your opponent will return a ball to you which is not high enough to smash and is too high to volley well. A ball like this is also likely to be fairly slow and to be 'hanging' in the air. The best shot to play is a volley, but in order to generate some pace on your return you should swing as you do for a groundstroke. This shot is called a drive volley and involves using a groundstroke action on a ball which has not bounced. The idea is to return the ball hard and deep into your opponent's court.

It is also possible to play a drive volley as a surprise shot from the back-court when your opponent is expecting you to play a groundstroke. You can then move quickly forwards to the net.

The shot is a mixture of two techniques so remember the following points when you are learning it:

1. The ball must be in the right position in relation to you. The height of it will vary, but is likely to be around head height. You must still make contact with it slightly in front and on the racket side (as for the basic volley).
2. The racket should be taken back early and then *swung* forwards as it would be for a groundstroke (but obviously much higher). Since the ball is played so high it will help to bring the ball down into court if the racket face is closed over the ball at impact. Otherwise the ball could be hit out well over the baseline.

The flight path of the ball for the drive volley.

FOREHAND · DRIVE · VOLLEY

The forehand drive volley. This shot, unlike the drop volley, employs a swing like a groundstroke, driving the ball deep, preferably with a slightly closed racket face.

opponent is at the net too, trying to volley past you. So the lob volley is another 'touch shot', needing firm wrist control and an open racket.

The basic principles of the lob volley are:

1. Keep the ball in the right place in relation to you.
2. Play the shot as you would the volley, with little or no backswing but with an open racket face to lift the ball high over your opponent. This will mean a slightly longer follow through than the basic volley. The shot will be easier to play if you bend your knees slightly.

The idea behind this shot is surprise. As the ball is lifted over his head your opponent will have to turn and chase it, so it also helps if you angle the ball. Having been lob-volleyed once, your opponent should be more wary of coming to the net in case it happens again.

The lob volley

Most volleys are played *down* into your opponent's court, but this is a volley which is sent high *up* into the air to land just inside the baseline in your opponent's court. The reason for this is because your

The path of the racket when playing the lob volley.

The flight path of the ball when playing the lob volley.

FOUR

IMPROVING YOUR
TACTICS

The essential tactics of the game were covered in Chapter Two and must form the basis of your match strategy. To remind you, they are:

1. Keep the ball in play.
2. Make your opponent run.
3. Keep a good position on court.

However, since this is exactly what your opponent is also trying to do, it may be useful to look at two other ideas.

1. Exploit a weakness.
2. Use surprise as a tactic.

These two tactics, combined with the additional strokes which were covered in the previous chapter, will improve your game.

EXPLOIT · A · WEAKNESS

Like any of us, your opponent will have some strokes which are better than others, and which he prefers to play. If you play on his weaker strokes then his returns will be less testing for you, and he will be put under greater mental pressure.

It may be that his playing style allows you to attack specific weak points. Alternatively he may like to play in a certain way — perhaps he prefers staying on the baseline or is a serve and volleyer. By using tactics which upset his preferred type of game, you can put pressure on him. Being strong in specific ways makes a player potentially weak in others, and any of these weaknesses can be used to your advantage.

Your first problem is to find out which your opponent's weaker strokes are, because you could lose a few vital games before you find out. You have one early chance, which is during the knock up before the match. During that short time you are trying to loosen up and perhaps calm your nerves, but it is also a good opportunity to see what clues your opponent gives you. The obvious one is whether he is better on the forehand or backhand. (Don't forget, of course, to check out whether he is right- or left-handed.) Does he like low or high bounces? Has he got a good first serve? What sort of second serve does he have? Does he volley well? You will certainly get a few ideas from the knock up. But be aware, some people play rather differently during the knock up than they do in the real match. It is much easier if you can find out something about your opponent beforehand. Perhaps you will be able to watch him play another match or even ask other players who know his game quite well.

Having found out as much as you can, you must work out a game plan. You should certainly aim to play on his weaker shots, especially on the 'big' points when the score is at a critical stage. If his second serve is weak, move in after the first one to increase the pressure on him to make the serve a little deeper. If he volleys well, try to hit deep to his baseline to keep him back and away from the net. The secret, though, is not to *overplay* his weakness. If one or two start to work well, his confidence will increase and the 'weakness' will become a strength.

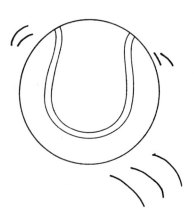

Your opponent's stroke play

Most players have a particular style of strokeplay which makes them vulnerable in certain situations. This is another reason why you need to know as much as possible about your opponent. Many current players enjoy hitting top-spin and have a strong forehand, which is helped by using the semi-western or western grip. The point to remember is that if a player has a Semi-Western or Western forehand then he finds it much more difficult to play balls hit wide of him or balls which stay low. On the other hand he positively enjoys balls which bounce up and give him plenty of opportunity for top-spin. If your opponent has a good top-spin forehand, and since it is almost impossible to go through a game without playing the ball to his forehand, it might help to keep the ball wide and low as these are the weak areas for that stroke.

If you have an opponent with a two-handed backhand who hits the ball very hard and is able to disguise the stroke very well, his weakness again will be the wide ball, because of his reduced reach.

Your opponent's style

The third area in which to look for a weakness is your opponent's actual style of play. Some players like to take their time and play the game at their own pace. They use the full time between points and at change-overs, and probably prefer playing at the baseline to coming to the net. Others like to 'get on with things' and probably play the serve and volley game. They will have difficulty with the baseline rallies which rely upon consistency, and the patient structuring of opportunities to win the point. It will be obvious to you that by speeding up the game against the first sort of player and slowing it down against the second you can exploit a weakness in their style and so put them under pressure. Players under pressure are more likely to make mistakes. In order to do this, however, you might have to change some of your own habits.

The baseliner who takes time to build up to a winning point should be forced to the net to volley. You will need to use the drop shot to bring him in and the lob to push him back. An alternative could be to get to the net yourself to volley the ball away, but baseliners can usually hit the ball deep and keep you back. You should try taking up the ball early on your groundstrokes to give him less time to recover. In Chapter Two we talked about hitting the ball on the groundstrokes as it was *dropping* for the second bounce. Taking the ball early means hitting it as it is *rising* from the bounce.

In order to do this you must remember the following things:

1. Shorten your backswing, because you will have less time to play the stroke, and as the ball is travelling faster you need less backswing.
2. Watch the ball right onto your racket, because the timing of the shot is different.
3. Keep your weight going forwards.
4. Perhaps bend your knees a little more.

Hitting the falling ball means the contact point is after the ball begins to drop for the second bounce.

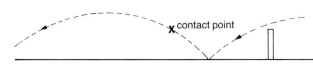

Hitting the ball early i.e. *as the ball rises from its first bounce.*

Another strategy against this style of play could be to serve and return wide to the angles, thus forcing your opponent out of court and opening up the court for you. The over-riding principle is to move your opponent around so that he does not have time to settle into a rhythm.

When playing against a serve and volley player you will want to adopt the opposite tactics. You have to find a way of stopping your opponent getting to the net. One answer could be to attack the serve, by hitting your service return early to cut down his time to get to the net. Alternatively hit the ball to the service line so that, as an incoming server, the ball lands at his feet and he is forced to hit it up. If you can lob the serve (quite a difficult thing to do!) the server will be discouraged from coming in to volley.

All these strategies are designed to stop the server moving from the baseline. If you force him to hit from the back of the court you will hope to increase the chance of an error as he continually looks for an opportunity to move forwards. If he does get to the volleying position you must lob, thus discouraging him from coming in quite so far again. Finally, if you get to the net yourself, you can volley in order to win the point.

All players have weaknesses and if you can discover what they are then you should play to them. If a player is strong in some areas he must be vulnerable in others. Theoretically there is a complete player, but thankfully you are unlikely to meet him in your club.

USE · SURPRISE

At any point, in either a match or a rally, your opponent will be expecting you to do certain things. Not playing the obvious is a strategy of confounding your opponent's expectations. The results of such a strategy are varied. You may simply win that point, (perhaps a vital one) or you may also create doubt in your opponent's mind. He will not know what you are going to do next and consequently he will be put under increased mental pressure, making it difficult for him to play well.

Not playing the obvious is based on three things:

1. You need an extended range of shots and variations if you are to play a surprise shot.
2. You need to read the game and to know when not to play the obvious.
3. You need to read the opposition to know what he is expecting or is likely to do.

Surprise shots

Often in a match the rallies seem to settle into a pattern. For example, two baseliners who hit top-spin groundstrokes will expect the ball to behave in a certain way. If one of them were to hit slice, his opponent would have to adjust very quickly to a different flight and bounce because he would not be prepared for the sliced return. When two players are moving each other backwards and forwards across the baseline, a rhythm is established. If one of them changes the pattern by going for the same side of the court again or by dropping the ball for a drop shot, his opponent is caught off guard. If players are volleying, a lob volley would be an unexpected stroke and would probably win the point. The art of not playing the obvious is clearly enhanced by your ability

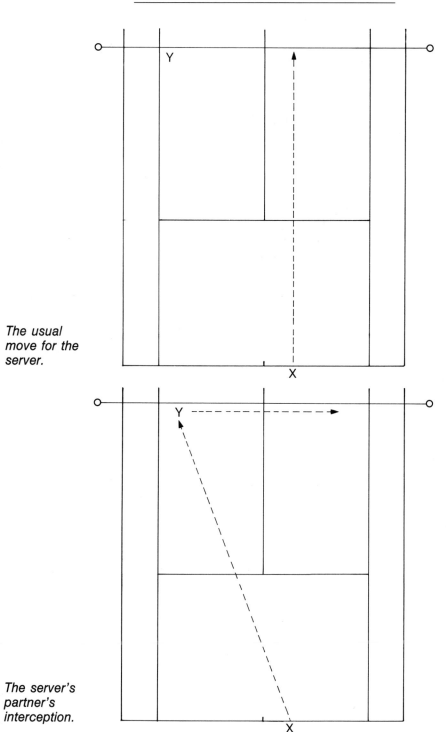

The usual move for the server.

The server's partner's interception.

to play different strokes and to use spin. The short-term gain is to win the rally, but the long-term gain is that your opponent will never quite know what to expect next.

Reading the game

It is not surprising that many matches seem to fall into a pattern, since most players will have some sort of game plan. But the player who can introduce an element of surprise at the right moment will unsettle his opponent and put himself in a stronger position. Such a strategy can been seen in doubles when the server's partner suddenly runs across and intercepts the return and the server moves forward to his team-mate's position. If the receivers are not expecting such a move they will be uncertain thereafter about returning the serve.

Reading the opposition

This is obviously linked to the strategy of reading the game. You need to take note of your opponent. Does he seem to be becoming more confident? Is he getting irritated by where and how you are hitting the ball, or by himself? Or is he becoming despondent? If he is becoming increasingly confident (probably because he is winning) then it is time to change your strategy and start playing the unexpected.

Steffi Graf and her famous forehand – timing is what makes this one of her best strokes. Although it is difficult to pick out one aspect of her game for particular praise. Her domination of the circuit in recent years points to her all-round excellence.

If you normally stay on the baseline, perhaps you should start to serve and volley, or chip and charge if receiving. If you have been allowing your opponent to hit all the angles start hitting the ball at him in the middle of the baseline. If he has been nearly hitting you off the court, try taking the pace off your returns and not giving him anything to hit. Any change in your tactics will at least have the benefit of bring doubt into his mind.

If your opponent is becoming despondent then you must remain confident and keep the ball in the court at all costs. Make *him* play the ball because in that mood he is more likely to make a mistake, and the more he makes, the more despondent he will become.

Of course you must remember to keep your feelings to yourself. Don't give your opponent a chance to take the same advantage of your mood that you are taking of his!

TENNIS

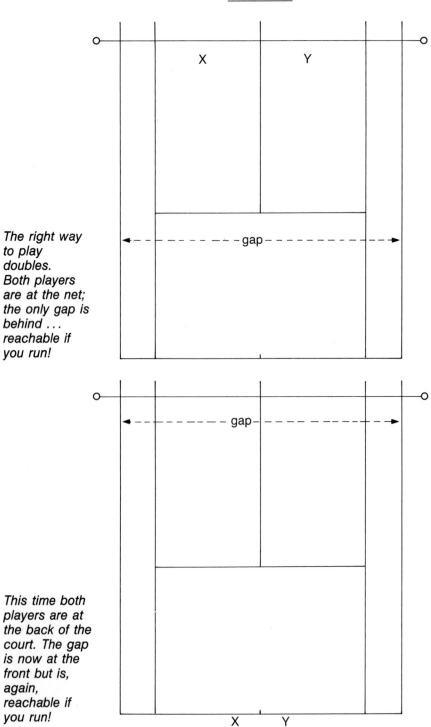

The right way to play doubles. Both players are at the net; the only gap is behind ... reachable if you run!

This time both players are at the back of the court. The gap is now at the front but is, again, reachable if you run!

DOUBLES · TACTICS

Obviously the tactics and strategies which we have considered so far apply equally well to doubles as to singles. But there are other tactics which are specific to the doubles game. Doubles is widely played in tennis clubs and it is worth considering the particular skills of playing the doubles game.

First it is a team game. This is a vital point to remember. You and your partner should be helping and encouraging each other as a partnership. You need to decide who should play in which court. Generally speaking the stronger player should receive service in the advantage (left hand) court. More important points are played into this service court which is why you need the better receiver and

returner of the serve there. In mixed doubles the man receives in this court and in men's or ladies doubles the stronger receiver plays there. However, if one player is left-handed, he or she will usually take the left court.

Part of the team play strategy is built around knowing who will hit which shot. For example, if the ball is hit down the centre then the player with the forehand in the centre usually hits it back. As the understanding between the partners develops so more possibilities of interception (taking your partner's stroke) arise. Constant communication between partners and encouragement of each other will lead to better understanding of this kind.

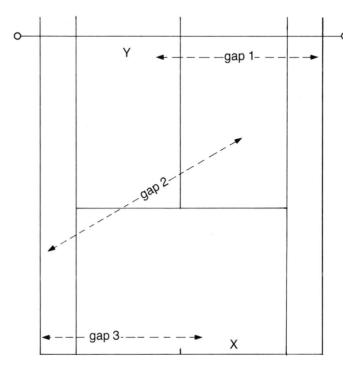

The wrong way to play doubles. One up, one back. The two small gaps (1 and 3) are reachable if you run but the large gap (2) is virtually impossible to reach.

It is important in doubles play that you should try to get to the net more quickly than your opponents. This applies to both of you. Try not to play a system with one up at the net and one back because it gives your opponents so many gaps into which to hit the ball.

If you can get to the net then you have the advantage of hitting the ball down while your opponents are forced to hit the ball up at you.

In doubles it is particularly important to try to win your service game. You must concentrate on getting the serve in and making your opponents play the ball. Take a little pace off the serve in order to get it deep in the court. This will keep your opponents back and give you that fraction of a second longer to join your partner at the net.

Leach and Pugh showing good doubles play; understanding, playing as a team, and attacking the net together.

FIVE

FACING THE

ELEMENTS

In this chapter we will consider how different court surfaces and different weather conditions can affect the game you want to play. Many club players take no notice of either and then cannot understand why they are losing when they ought to be winning.

COURT · SURFACES

One way in which tennis differs from most other games is that it is played on a variety of surfaces, as well as indoors and outdoors. The court can be made of clay or shale, of grass or artificial grass, of wood or plastic, of cement or tarmac. Most club players, particularly when they play matches against other clubs, will find themselves playing on different surfaces throughout the season. Different players are more successful on different surfaces, and this applies to you, as a club player, as much as it does to world class professionals.

The differences between playing on a good grass court as opposed to playing on tarmac, cement or shale are fundamental.

It is important that you understand the differences for two reasons. The first is to understand what the ball is likely to do

and the second, with that in mind, to know how to play on such surfaces to your advantage.

Fast courts

On fast courts, such as grass, the ball stays low when it bounces and the serve, in particular, will be an important shot. You have much less time to get to the ball and to play your shots. The volley is another important and match-winning shot on a fast court. If you are able to serve and volley well, you will probably like playing on fast surfaces.

Slow courts

At the other end of the scale are the slow surfaces like shale (sometimes called blase), tarmac courts with a loose top dressing, and many all-weather surfaces.

On slow surfaces the ball bounces higher as well as slower. Consequently you have more time to get to the ball and hit it. It is more difficult to 'put the ball

Virginia Wade, forced onto the back foot for the forehand drive during one of her last singles matches at Wimbledon in 1985. Her greatest triumph was, of course, the Wimbledon singles title in Jubilee Year, 1977.

away', so the serve and volleyer does not have the same advantage on these courts. Longer rallies are usual and you will need to build your way to a winning position using patience and good ball placement.

Medium-pace courts

There are some surfaces which can be called medium-pace courts. Many indoor surfaces, such as carpet, rubberised surfaces and synthetic grass, and some all-weather courts, fall into this category. The ball bounces up, but not as high as it does on a slow court. Spinning the ball and playing a good volleying game are useful assets on a medium-pace court.

WEATHER · CONDITIONS

If you always play indoors then this section need not concern you, as your only problem will be heat. If you play outdoors, you need to think about how to cope in strong sunny conditions and in windy and wet conditions.

Sunny conditions

The position of the sun in relation to the court can be a problem, especially if you have to serve or smash into it. If your opponent is looking into a strong sun the lob is a useful weapon. If you play doubles with a left-hander you may be able to organize your order of serving so that neither of your serves into the sun. If you are playing in high temperatures, remember that the balls will seem lighter and 'fly' more on hot than on cold days. You must take this into account when serving or hitting to a full length.

Wind

Windy conditions are, perhaps, more difficult than sun. The wind may be gusting, which makes play very difficult because it is unpredictable. If it is blowing continuously down the court, you will have to work out how to get to the net at one end and stay back at the other. Top-spin will help keep the ball in from one end, while slice could give you length from the other. A side wind is even more of a problem, but it can be used to help you angle the ball or to move a slice serve even further out of court. But don't forget that your opponent can also use this tactic to his advantage.

Rain

Wet conditions will have an effect on the tennis balls. They will seem heavier and if they get wet they will become more difficult to hit. The court will also play differently in the rain. The ball will not bounce as high and the surface may become slippery. Playing in such conditions is hard work, and the best advice is to win your match as quickly as possible, get off court and go for a nice warm shower!

SIX

PRACTICE

AND

EXERCISE

In this chapter we will look at the principles of practice and suggest several exercises which you can use to develop your strokes.

PRACTICE

For practice to have any real or lasting benefit it has to have a purpose. Just hitting a tennis ball, although it may be fun, will not make you into a better tennis player. If you want to reach a higher standard in your stroke production so that you can play a higher quality match, and win against better players, you need to view practice sessions in a more purposeful light. In other words you need to aim for quality as well as quantity.

Quality of performance is a great asset in your matches. If you know that a particular stroke is sound, because you have executed it many times in practice, then the tension of the match should not cause your stroke production to crumble.

Armed with that confidence, you can concentrate on your tactics for winning rather than on trying to avoid a particular shot. Inevitably, there will be days when your whole game works better than it does on others, but that does not detract from quality practice.

Grooving your strokes

To be effective your strokes need to be grooved, which means that you can rely on them being nearly the same every time you use them. They also need to be adaptable, so that they can respond to the odd occasion when the bounce is not true or a gust of wind blows the ball off course.

To achieve this grooving, you must first of all be sure that a stroke is technically sound. Here a qualified coach will help. You then need to practise it in a structured situation so that you can repeat it again and again. This structured situation will be a drill or exercise which allows repetition. As you improve your ability to complete the stroke, then the drill or exercise should be changed to increase the pressure and see if you can maintain the quality of performance. At this point it is sensible to put the stroke into a game context by including it in a series of different shots, in an exercise resembling what actually happens in a game. You should be able to repeat your stroke and maintain your quality of performance.

Footwork and movement

Practising your footwork and movement around the court is vital. After all, it is not much use hitting perfect shots if you never get to the ball in the first place. Movement off the ball and good footwork during the stroke are essential and you should not forget that aspect in practice.

Pressure training

Practising at a level above that which you will play in matches is a good idea. It is often called pressure training. Such training makes you move and hit tennis balls at a greater speed than you are likely to have to do in a match. If you can achieve quality of performance in pressure training then you should be able to cope well with the match. Practising with a friend, or perhaps two friends, not only makes practice more fun and enjoyable, but enables you to help each other with any problems.

Most practice, of course, needs at least two people (unless you have a ball machine) and ideally you should have a partner of similar standard to yourself. You certainly need one who is interested to work at quality practice with you.

Finally, good quality practice for a short space of time is more beneficial than random hitting followed by a game.

EXERCISES

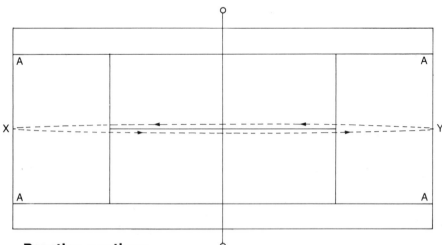

Practice routines
Practice 1: rallying to a length consistently; 2: rallying forehands consistently, and 3: rallying backhands. Vary the shots with back-spin and slice and then practise hitting one of the four A targets.

PRACTICE · AND · EXERCISE

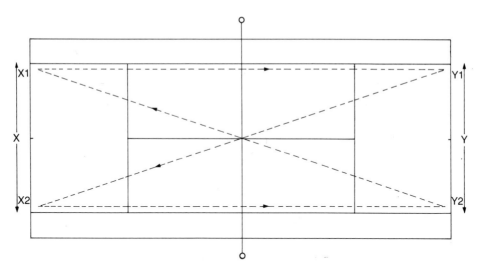

X rallies straight from X1 to Y1,
Y then returns cross court to X2,
X2 returns straight to Y2 who then returns
cross court to X1 ... and so on. Reverse
the routine so that X then gets to practise
the cross-court strokes.

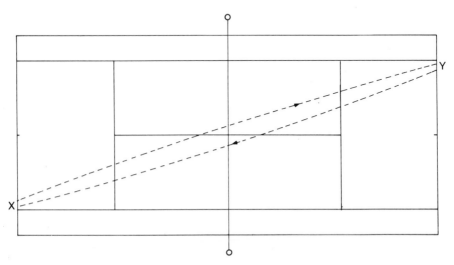

Rally forehand-to-forehand across court.
Repeat from the opposite corner for
backhand practice.

TENNIS

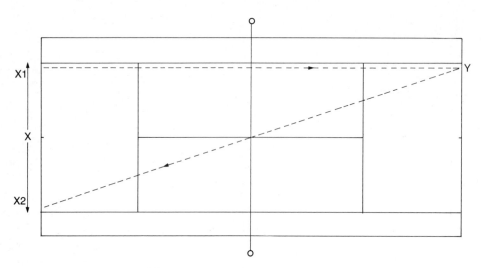

Player Y stays stationary and returns either to position X1 or X2. X must always return to the stationary player Y.

Martina Navratilova is still one of the world's leading players and her ability to attack from almost anywhere on the court has been one of her trademarks.

TENNIS

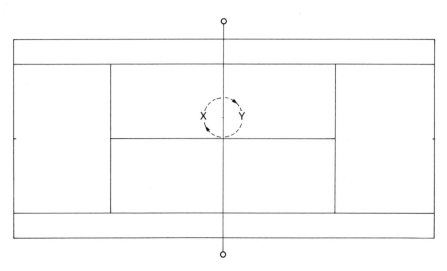

*Follow close-in to the net. This exercise
will help to improve your footwork.*

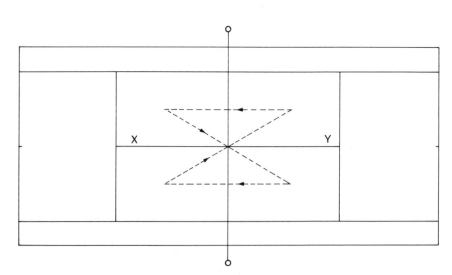

*Another volleying exercise. Player Y
always returns the ball straight while
player X returns diagonally.*

PRACTICE · AND · EXERCISE

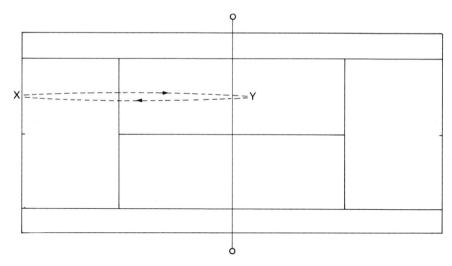

Player X plays a groundstroke to Y who volleys back to X to play another groundstroke ... and so on.

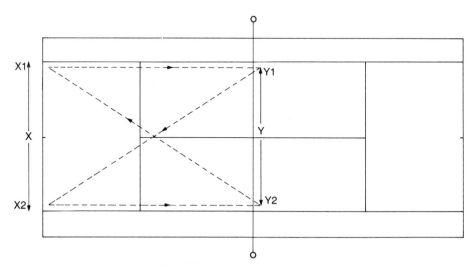

Another 'volley-to-groundstroke' practice routine: Player X always hits straight while the player at the net, Y, returns diagonally.

TENNIS

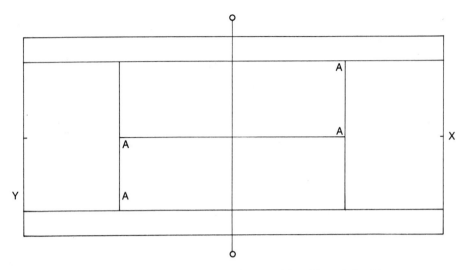

Practice serving from the singles position X and doubles position Y. Practice second serves as well as first serves, serving each alternately. Also practice serving to hit A targets to improve the accuracy of your serve.

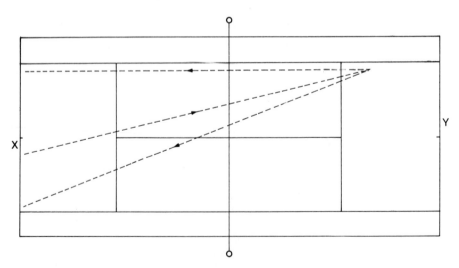

Combining stokes – serve/return of serve
1. Serve–return consistently.
2. Serve to target–return to target consistently.
3. Vary serving target–vary return target.
4. Serve–return, play out rally – score.
5. Serve–return, play out rally – but only score on volley.

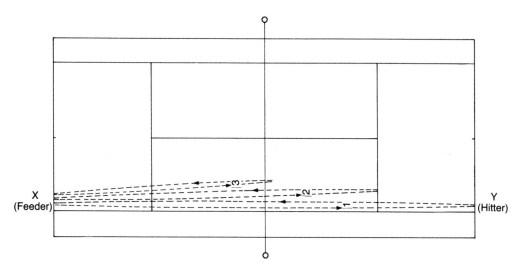

Combining strokes – full length drives/approach shot to volley.

Player X feeds a sequence of three balls. The first is hit deep. The second is hit to the service line and the third to a volley at the net. Player Y has to move forward to play shots 2 and 3. After this opening sequence has been played, X can vary the sequence.

TENNIS

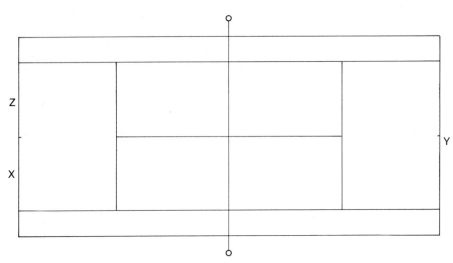

Pressure training
Two versus one with all three players on
the baseline. Players Z and X try to beat
Y by playing the ball anywhere into his
court. Y should aim for a total shot score.

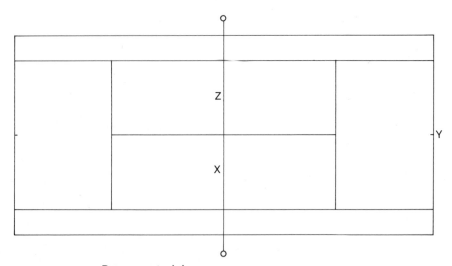

Pressure training
Two versus one: Players X and Z are at
the net; Y is on the baseline. The object
of the two players at the net is to reduce
player Y's time to play the shot. Y should
aim for a total shot score.

Edberg – the master of serve.

TENNIS

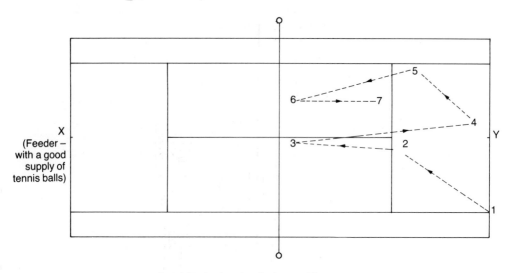

A typical circuit of shots. There are many different combinations and here is one example.
Player Y is fed a sequence of balls in a set order. This example is: 1 Deep drive; 2 Approach; 3 Volley; 4 Retrieval; 5 Approach; 6 Volley; 7 Smash.
Aim to return: (a) consistently and (b) in timed sequence.

SEVEN

FITNESS
FOR TENNIS

What do you understand by fitness? You are probably aware of the need for physical fitness, but have you also considered mental fitness? You will need both as a tennis player.

WHY · TO · GET · FIT

Why be concerned with fitness? Anyone can play tennis – you only need to visit the local courts during Wimbledon fortnight to know that! The contrast, however, between that level of tennis and Wimbledon itself, is enormous. One of the differences is undoubtedly the ability of top players to continue to play at a high level for a long period of time, sometimes when it is very hot. They could not do so if they were not physically fit. The demands that tennis makes on the body are so varied that tennis players are the equal of athletes in any other sport. Some have an almost 'unnatural', natural advantage. Borg, for example, has an incredibly slow and strong heart beat. You, as an aspiring club player, will find that if you can improve your level of fitness your ability to play well in a match or practice session will improve.

HOW · TO · GET · FIT

Many people have a happy notion that they can be physically fit by jogging, eating healthy food, not smoking and so on. Of course these things do improve your fitness in a general way, but unfortunately, the physical fitness you need for sport is specific. Jogging, walking, swimming or cycling will all help you feel better and enable you to take part in physical activity, but if you wish to be fit for a particular sport, your fitness training should usually be geared directly towards that. You must decide which aspects of general fitness are particularly necessary for what you want to do. Then you must devise a training programme. As a tennis player, however, you are lucky (depending on how you see it) in that you will need to work at every aspect of your fitness in order to succeed because all the components of fitness will be vital to your game in some way.

There are four components of physical fitness – often referred to as the Four S's:

1. Suppleness (or flexibility).
2. Speed.
3. Strength.
4. Stamina (or endurance).

As a tennis player you need to develop a good base level in each. In addition, your fitness training programme needs to be evenly balanced in the development of the four components. You are likely to be more advanced in one component than another and so may think you do not need to work quite so hard in that area. But if you did work at it then you could make it a great asset of your game. For example, Steffi Graf has incredible natural speed that could perhaps have made her a successful track athlete. She has used her speed to help her become an outstanding tennis player. Boris Becker, on the other hand, has great strength, but has needed to work hard on his speed and mobility to become the accomplished player that he is.

A second factor to bear in mind in your training programme is that there will be times, perhaps just before a tournament, when you need to cut back in some areas. Stamina training, for example, is a long-term training exercise and should not be done just before a competition.

Suppleness

Another word for this is flexibility and either term refers to the range of movements in a joint within your body. As your tennis improves you will find that having the ability to reach the wider, higher or shorter balls is a great asset and may well make the difference between winning and losing. To do this you need to be very flexible in all of your joints, and so your training programme will need to include work for extra suppleness.

Speed

Your ability to move quickly is linked to your agility. It relies on your being able both to move your joints quickly and to move your whole body around the court.

Obviously speed of movement in

particular joints is important in matches and enables you to respond effectively, and get to the ball quickly. Tennis is a game involving fast movement around quite a small area, with many changes of direction. You will therefore need to improve your agility if you are to compete with better players.

Strength

Tennis players need to be strong for what can be a physically demanding game. They need to have strong legs to cope with the running and the repetitive bending and stretching; strong arms in order to use the racket well over a period of time; and strong back and hip muscles for actions such as serving.

The power in Steffi Graf's legs gives some indication as to how much speed she can generate around the court.

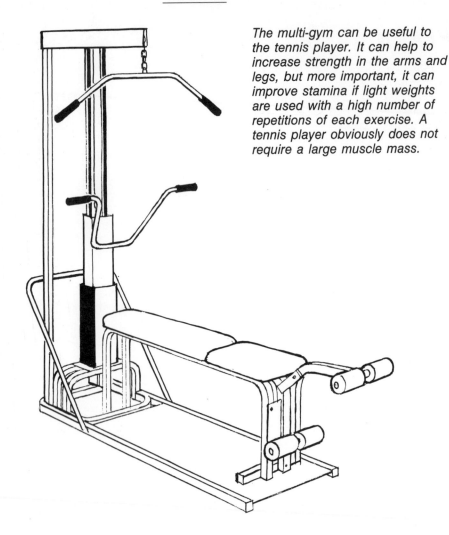

The multi-gym can be useful to the tennis player. It can help to increase strength in the arms and legs, but more important, it can improve stamina if light weights are used with a high number of repetitions of each exercise. A tennis player obviously does not require a large muscle mass.

Stamina

If you have watched tennis on television you will know that in the major championships, when five-set matches are played, players can be on court for three to four hours. Clearly their ability to continue to play high-quality tennis for such a long period is indicative of their stamina or endurance. Training to develop this component of fitness is clearly essential to the top players who never know how long they are going to be on court. Even club players can lose matches, especially on hot, sunny days, if they get tired and can't play their shots because they have run out of stamina.

There are two types of stamina and the tennis player needs both. The first is the short-term stamina needed for bursts of activity such as serving or playing a rally. The second is the long-term endurance which is needed to keep you going through long matches.

PLANNING · A · TRAINING · PROGRAMME

It is up to you to decide how fit you want to be – which dictates how much training you want to do. Obviously the other areas of your life, apart from playing tennis, will affect such decisions. If your ambitions stop at becoming a reasonable club player, you may decide not to do any training, but if you want to play at a better level than that, you must work on your physical fitness. Half an hour three times a week would benefit you a great deal. You can work out your own training programme, bearing in mind the principles below, or you may prefer to go to your local sports centre, join a class, and get a qualified instructor to help devise a programme especially tailored to your needs and sport.

No matter what form of training you engage in you should bear in mind these principles:

1. *Always* warm up before starting training and warm down afterwards.
2. Take your match or tournament programme into account when planning your programme.
3. Do not change your exercise just before a match, since you may become stiff from a change in routine.
4. Remember that stamina training is long-term.
5. Don't mix suppleness and speed training with technique training.
6. Do suppleness and speed training before strength and stamina work.
7. Always do strength training with weights under the supervision of an expert.
8. You can include stamina training as a part of skill training, for example as part of your pressure training exercises.

Warming up

The reason for warming up at all is to get your body ready for physical activity. When you take any form of exercise you need to be warm and to have the blood flowing through the working muscles. If you don't warm up then you could well pull muscles and stretch ligaments. The warm up should consist of jogging gently for three or four minutes and perhaps doing some skipping, followed by stretching exercises to get the muscles warm and ready for vigorous activity. Stretch large muscle groups first, before moving to individual muscles.

At the end of the warm up you should be feeling alert and fit for activity. If instead you are feeling exhausted, then something is wrong!

TENNIS

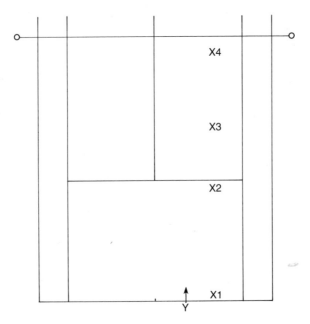

Sprinting practice. Start sprinting from position Y, pick up the ball at X1, return it to Y then collect X2 and return to Y and so on.

Speed training

To a certain extent your ability to move quickly is something you are born with. Some people, for example, have a faster reaction time than others. You will realise that your ability to react to a fast serve, or to the unexpected drop shot, is an important feature of being a good tennis player, as is your ability to move quickly over the tennis court. Both these skills can be improved with training.

It is important to make reaction training relevant to the game of tennis, by, for instance, practising the return of a fast serve.

Improving your speed of movement, on the other hand, can be achieved with more general exercises. Practise **sprinting** quickly across the width of the court, then two courts, before turning and sprinting back. You can also try **potato races**. These are short sprints with bending and turning. Space several tennis balls across the court. Sprint to pick up the first ball, bring it back to the starting point, then sprint for the second ball and bring it back, and so on. Time your runs, and try gradually to cut down your time.

As a third form of speed training you can **run** at an even pace for a fixed short distance and then sprint at full speed over the same distance. Repeat several times. Remember that you need to give yourself recovery time between each period of sprinting speed work. The recovery time is necessary because your muscles contract rapidly and tire quickly. They need time to rest. As your speed training improves, so your muscle groups become stronger and better able to cope with the energy requirement of fast movements.

Suppleness training

The aim of training for suppleness should be to increase your range of movement and to reduce the possibility of injury. You use all the joints and muscle groups in your body when you play tennis, so your training programme should also use as many of them as possible.

Stretching exercises are for muscles. Your legs, arms, stomach and back all have large muscle groups, and your exercises should last 10 to 15 seconds for each group of muscles. Stretch for 10 to 15 seconds, release slowly and then repeat 5 to 20 times. The stretching should be smooth, not jerked, and should reach the point where it is slightly uncomfortable. You should then hold the stretch for a few seconds before relaxing slowly. If you can relax the rest of your body while you stretch each part it will help the exercise.

Spend some part of your flexibility training on these **mobility exercises** for your joints:

1. Arm circling to loosen your shoulder and elbow joints.
2. Head rotation to mobilise your neck joint and muscles.
3. Trunk circling to help your hip and lower back.
4. Leg and ankle circling to help your hips, knee and ankles.

Apart from contributing to your tennis training, 10 to 15 minutes a day of these exercises will be good for general physical fitness.

Strength training

If your muscles are stronger they will be able to work more effectively and for longer periods without tiring. Strength training should be specific to the sport you are playing, because certain muscle groups are more important in certain sports. As a tennis player you specifically need strength in your arms, trunk and legs. If you are working on your own it would be sensible to get advice on a strength training programme from an expert.

Bench presses increase the power of arms and chest: clearly, the tennis stroke is not given its power solely by the arm.

A strength training programme could use some **weight training**, but if you do engage in this then it *must be under supervision*. Alternatively, you can use a **circuit-type exercise** programme. This type of strength training incorporates a series of exercises in sequence which you need to repeat a certain number of times. As you develop your fitness so you are able either to increase the number of exercises or to perform the same number in a shorter time. Either way you can measure your improvement. A successful circuit should incorporate the following exercises:

1. Bend and stretch.
2. Sit ups – straight and diagonal.
3. Back arches.
4. Burpees.
5. Press-ups.

These exercises will help to develop strength in all your muscle groups and should be done in succession. Do three circuits, noting your time. When you can do this easily, increase the number of each exercise as shown in the following programme.

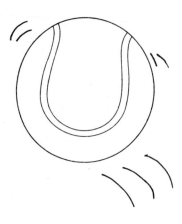

Bend and Stretch (*10 times initially, then 15, then 20*) Stand with your legs straight and your feet shoulder-width apart. Place both hands on the ground between your legs as far back as possible. Then raise your arms above your head and at the same time push your hips forward and shoulders back.

Sit-ups (*9 times initially, then 12, then 15*) Lie flat on your back with your hands behind your head and your knees slightly bent. If possible, it is best to anchor your feet under an immovable object. From that horizontal position, sit up touching your knees with your elbows and then return to the lying position. As you get more used to the exercise, start turning your back as you pull yourself forward and touch your left knee with your right elbow and then vice versa.

Back arches (*10 times initially, then 15, then 20*) Lie on your front with your arms behind your back. Lift your head, shoulders, and chest off the ground as high as possible by arching your back. Hold for a couple of seconds and then return to the lying position.

Burpees (*10 times initially, then 15, then 20*) Stand with your legs straight and with your feet shoulder-width apart. Drop to a squat position, supporting yourself on your hands. At the same time, push your legs out to the press-up position. Return your feet to the squat position and then stand up straight again.

Press-ups (*6 times initially, then 9, then 12*) Lie on your front, with your body straight, and support yourself on your toes, keeping your arms straight. Lower your whole body, keeping it straight, to the ground, and then repeat. Women should do this exercise with their knees on the ground.

Stamina training

Like strength training, stamina or endurance training must be done over a period of time and certainly not immediately before a tournament.

Long-term endurance will be improved through training such as running, swimming and cycling, when you increase your heart rate and keep it at that level for a period of time. You do not need to work to the point of exhaustion but three half-hour sessions a week would be a good starting point.

Short-term endurance can be improved by the sort of circuit training exercises described above for strength training.

Warming down

When you have finished a training session it is sensible to repeat the gentle jogging and stretching exercises you did at the beginning. Then have a shower and relax!

MENTAL · FITNESS

You can work hard to develop your strokes and improve your fitness by means of practical, physical activities, but the mental aspects of playing tennis are just as important. It is very difficult to win if you are in the wrong frame of mind or unable to concentrate. If you feel a little nervous, that is a good thing, as the adrenalin starts to flow and you will probably play a bit better.

Concentration is vital. In any match many things can take away your concentration, but only one thing can get it back – you! Sound match preparation will help.

You must aim to start the match physically well prepared, equipped with rackets, comfortable shoes and clothes, and with a well prepared match plan.

From that point on you must *concentrate*, first and foremost on the ball and on the point you are playing. Don't worry what your opponent is doing. Forget the last bad shot – it's over and you can't do anything about it, even if it was a vital point. If you worry about it, or let a bad line call upset you, then you'll lose even more points. Don't even think about the next point. Many matches have been lost by players thinking they have won and then not playing the final point well. Concentrate on the point you are playing and what you are going to do with the ball. You know what your match plan is and you should stick to it unless you start to lose badly. Remember the main aim in tennis is to get the ball over the net and into court. Your opponent then has the problem of getting it back.

TENNIS

Sometimes concentration can be difficult, especially when all sorts of irritating distractions occur. Why not practise these situations and see if you can still maintain your level of concentration? Get your practice partner to make bad calls or give the wrong score – and don't get angry. Get people to make a noise on the next court or nearby, and still concentrate. Have other players hit a ball across your court and keep your mind on the ball you're hitting. Play with another racket and forget that it isn't your own – and don't blame the racket when you make mistakes. These are all everyday occurrences in the game of tennis and getting used to coping with them in practice situations will help you when they happen to you at match-point in a tournament final! If you can concentrate in the face of provocation in practice you will be much better prepared for the same situation in a match. But the most important thing you must do is to believe in yourself and never give up.

EIGHT

TENNIS
INJURIES

It is possible, despite all your best efforts, that you will get injured on the tennis court. Even if you have warmed up well and are fit, it is still possible that injuries will happen. Some injuries occur irrespective of training. Although it is not always possible to prevent injuries and accidents, it is possible to reduce the likelihood of their happening, and to be prepared if they do. Remember these points:

1. Make sure you are fit to play and always warm up.
2. Make sure you have the correct equipment.
3. Try not to play if you are tired.
4. Carry your own first aid kit.
5. Seek expert medical help as quickly as possible after receiving an injury.
6. Go to a sports injuries clinic if your doctor recommends it.
7. Take expert advice before playing again. If you play too soon you will be back where you started.

Essentially the tennis player will be concerned with soft tissue injuries. It is quite unusual for tennis players to break arms or legs on the court, but muscles, tendons, ligament sprains and abrasion injuries are common.

One thing you must bear in mind with joint injuries is that they usually require a lot of rest or even total immobilization until cured. So don't be impatient if you suffer such an injury.

Tennis elbow

This is the most infamous of tennis injuries. It is an inflammation of the tendons in the elbow and is usually felt particularly on the backhand. It is an injury which generally takes a long time to clear up and the remedies are various. The cause is often a puzzle to the sufferer but

it is important to try to establish the cause if you can. If it is a result of poor technique then the cure is obvious, even if it isn't easy to put into practice. Many of these injuries are the result of the wrong size grip (see Chapter One) or incorrect stringing tension. Go to an expert coach and stringer for advice.

Some people wear a fore-arm splint to stop the pain while others have cortisone injections into the inflamed joint. An extreme solution is surgery.

Shoulder joints

Inflammation of the shoulder joint can be caused by excessive or hard serving.

Chris Evert was one of the game's finest baseline players and had pinpoint accuracy, even from the back of the court.

Knee joints

Injuries to knee joints are frequent in tennis because of the constant bending, stretching and twisting movements, but also because the knees frequently have to be used as 'shock absorbers'. Wearing the right shoes is essential. For example, if you are playing indoors, wear a smoother solid shoe. Heavily ribbed soles tend to cause your feet to become static and if your body moves against 'fixed' feet, your knees can suffer.

Ankle joints

Sprained ankles are a frequent injury in most sports but again good footwear can help to prevent them.

The key to a good shoe is always close-fitting support, to alleviate the constant jarring and turning of the foot during a game.

Wrist joints

Sprains are not that common but some tennis players have problems with inflamed tendons in the wrist. These are sometimes caused by excessive play, but can also occur from using the wrong racket or from incorrect stringing. Poor technique is another possible cause of inflamed tendons in the wrist joints.

Back injuries

Certain strokes in tennis are known to cause back problems, especially in the lower back (or lumbar region). The top-spin serve is an obvious possible culprit and the two-handed backhand can put more pressure on the lumbar region than the single-handed one. Many players suffer back problems from time to time.

Tendon injuries

Damage can take place to tendons for two reasons – either because of prolonged over-use or because of sudden unexpected stress. Tendon injuries can take a long time to heal.

Achilles tendon injuries can vary from a complete severance of the tendon to inflammation and pain. The former requires immediate hospitalization and surgery.

Inflammation of the Achilles tendon can again be caused by poor footwear, either from excessive jarring or from heel tabs which actually rub the tendon. Choose your shoes very carefully (see Chapter One).

Muscle injuries

Muscle injuries can occur for exactly the same reason as those to tendons – continuous aggravation or sudden unexpected stress. The muscle will hurt

American Aaron Krickstein losing in the fourth round (to Becker) at Wimbledon, 1989; clearly, the heavily strapped left leg didn't help. Cartilage breakdown is as much a threat to the tennis player as it is to the soccer player.

and restrict movement. Treatment for muscle injuries will normally include gentle movement but *not* the movement that caused it in the first place. As with all other injuries you should not try to play tennis again until it is cured.

Cramp

Cramp is a sudden and violent pain caused by muscles contracting in spasm. It can occur in the stomach, but more often than not it attacks the legs and feet. The affected muscle should be stretched in order to reduce the spasm but sometimes you need someone else to do it for you. Eating immediately before any strenuous activity can also be a cause of cramp, so be careful. (Though starving yourself for too long before a match will leave you listless, particularly if you have insufficient carbohydrate).

The causes of cramp are various but often include tiredness or loss of body salt. Either can occur in a long match, especially in heat. A good level of fitness will help, and in hot conditions you should keep your fluid level up during a match by taking frequent sips of water or perhaps fruit juice.

Blisters

These are classed as minor injuries, but they can have results as serious as those from a major muscle tear or tendon injury. They usually occur on your racket hand or your feet. If one (or more) appears on your racket hand then you will need to tape your fingers or have a couple of plasters over the blister. If it is very large, you could use a sterilised needle gently to press out the fluid, provided you then cover it with a sterile dressing. At least then you can continue to play.

A blister on your feet is more of a problem. Try soaking your feet in surgical spirit to harden them up. Make sure your shoes fit and that you wear two pairs of absorbent socks to prevent the blister recurring.

Cuts and grazes

If you fall on hard courts or even on artificial grass courts you may cut or burn yourself. If you do, clean the wound with an antiseptic dressing and cover it if necessary.

NINE

PROFESSIONAL
STYLE

Just as you, the club player, have to adapt to the varying surfaces, so does the professional tennis player, as he moves from tournament to tournament. Most professional players have strengths and weaknesses in their game which means that they play better on some surfaces than others. As a general rule a serve-and-volley player is more likely to succeed on a fast surface like grass, whereas the strong baseline player with solid groundstrokes may win more frequently on slower hard courts.

However, occasionally players come along who are exceptions to all the rules of probability. Bjorn Borg, for example, won Wimbledon five times in a row but he was not a serve-and-volleyer. However, what he did have was a variety of superb groundstrokes and an ability to beat the server. Jimmy Connors has also been a Wimbledon Champion and has played many memorable matches on the grass there, but again he is not a serve-and-volleyer. Hard, slower courts are supposed to suit the baseliner but in the 1989 French Open final Stefan Edberg lost narrowly to Michael Chang over five sets, even though Edberg is a fine exponent of serve-and-volley tactics.

Most world class players have distinctive playing styles which come to be identified with them. Borg's hallmark, for example, was a superb two-handed top-spin backhand which won him many points and matches. More recently Boris Becker's serve, Edberg's volleys and Steffi Graf's forehand have come to be judged as superb strokes.

TENNIS

Sometimes it is a player's particular ability which singles him or her out. Steffi Graf's speed around the court, for example, allows her to return many balls as winners where other players would merely be able to get the ball back. John McEnroe's touch play and ability to disguise his intentions mean that his opponents are frequently left guessing and unable to reach the ball. There is no doubt that as a tennis player he has the touch of genius and sometimes it is difficult to see how he manufactures a particular shot.

Ivan Lendl's fitness and will to win enable him to raise his game when his opponents are wilting. Martina Navratilova has a tremendous ability to attack her opponent's returns from all parts of the court, and Chris Evert is famous for the accuracy of her returns, especially from the baseline.

One of Boris Becker's greatest assets is his strength. You only have to watch him serve to appreciate how much power he generates.

STROKES · OF · THE · TOP · PLAYERS

Boris Becker's serve

Becker's first serve is an awesome shot. It has tremendous power and is hit very hard. As with any serve, the speed of the racket head immediately prior to impact is crucial, but because Becker is so strong he is able to channel both his own power and that of the racket head speed into his serve. Obviously such a serve counts most on grass and this is a major reason why he has been so successful at Wimbledon, without dominating the circuit on other surfaces.

Steffi Graf's forehand

This is classed by many tennis pundits as a superb, if individual, stroke. Again, as in Becker's serve, the ball is struck very hard with magnificent timing. That timing is helped considerably by Steffi Graf's speed around the court and her anticipation, which give her that fraction more time to prepare for the shot.

Stefan Edberg's serve and volley

Stefan Edberg is famed for his volleys which win many points, but they are the second half of his repertoire. He is a serve and volley player and it is his serve which allows him to get to the net in order to hit the first volley so well. His second serve, a wonderful top-spin, is among the best in the game at the moment.

At the net Martina is exceptionally strong.

Service returns

All the top players aim to win their service games consistently, and unlike many club players, they mainly succeed in this. But in order to win matches they must also win their opponent's service game. This obviously requires the ability to return the ball well, to keep it low and to try to pass the incoming server. Jimmy Connors who hits the ball flat and hard (that in itself is quite unusual) is a fine exponent of good service returns as is Mats Wilander.

LEARNING · FROM · THE · PROFESSIONALS

So what can the club player learn from watching the professionals? Certainly it is interesting and helpful to watch a player who is particularly sound in a certain stroke. However, this is often the result of some particular technique or asset which is peculiar to that player, and which it is very difficult for the average club player to emulate. John McEnroe's service action, for example, is very much his own and is a stroke which he has perfected. To copy it would be nearly impossible.

Mats Wilander shows how to return the serve, even on a wide-angled ball.

Nonetheless, there are several things that the club player can learn from the professional player. It is important, first of all to realise that the basics of stoke production, which we talked about in Chapter Two, are the same whoever you are and whatever your level of play. The second lesson to be gained is that the professionals have got to the top by hard work and attention to detail. It takes dedicated effort for them to develop and refine their strokes, and to achieve the level of fitness needed to play long matches at such a high standard of performance.

Ivan Lendl and Martina Navratilova are examples of players with the determination to reach an exceptional degree of fitness, and both work extremely hard to do so. Of course it is necessary to have the talent, but any amount of talent will be wasted without a high level of fitness, and an over-riding desire to succeed.

John McEnroe is probably one of the finest players at disguising his shots – even his serve.

TESTING TIME

A series of question, and answers, to see how much you have learned on the foregoing pages.

1. Which is the best grip to adopt for playing either the forehand or backhand volley without changing your grip?
   (a) Continental grip
   (b) Service grip
   (c) Chopper grip

2. With the semi-western grip does the racket face need to be:
   (a) Slightly closed
   (b) Slightly open
   (c) Square to the ball at impact

3. When playing a forehand shot with a Continental grip, approximately how high should the ball be when you make contact with it:
   (a) Above waist high
   (b) At a point between your knee and waist
   (c) Below knee high

4. When playing the backhand, either one- or two-handed, where should the ball be in relation to your front foot at the moment of impact?
   (a) Slightly in front of it
   (b) Slightly behind it
   (c) In line with it

5. If your opponent plays a stroke to you that starts with his racket-head in a low position, but finishes in a high follow-through, does this indicate he has played:
   (a) a topspin forehand
   (b) a sidespin forehand
   (c) a backspin forehand

6. What is the ideal volleying position?
   (a) Three feet from the net
   (b) Six feet from the net
   (c) 10 feet from the net

7. In a game of doubles where should the receiver's partner ideally stand?
   (a) About three feet from the net
   (b) On the side line
   (c) On the baseline

8. After the completion of serve and return in a game of doubles where is the ideal position for two players of the same side to adopt?
   (a) One close to the net and the other at the back of the court diagonally opposite
   (b) One close to the net and the other at the back of the court immediately behind
   (c) Next to each other, either on the baseline or up at the net

9. Which of the following would you adopt in order to put slice on your serve?
   (a) Turn your body more to the left
   (b) Throw the ball up slightly in front and to the right of you
   (c) Close the racket face at impact

10. Why is it advisable not to put spin on the ball when volleying?
    (a) Because it slows the shot down and gives your opponent more chance of recovery
    (b) It is likely to produce a less accurate shot
    (c) There is a likelihood of overhitting the ball

11. If your opponent is a good volleyer, which is the best stroke to play against him?
    (a) Forehand drive
    (b) Lob
    (c) Drop shot

12. What is the key element in playing the drop shot?
    (a) Take the speed off the ball
    (b) Keep your eyes on the ball at all times
    (c) Have control of the racket

13. When smashing, what should you do to balance your racket arm and body?
    (a) Make sure your feet are behind the ball
    (b) Make sure your non-racket arm is outstretched
    (c) Bend the knee of your front leg slightly

14. What is the ideal height of the ball when playing the drive volley?
    (a) Head high
    (b) Chest high
    (c) Knee high

15. If a player has a semi-western or western forehand which *two* of the following shots is he more likely to have difficulty with?
    (a) Balls hit wide of him
    (b) Balls hit low
    (c) Balls played high

16. Would a good serve and volley player prefer playing on:
    (a) Clay
    (b) Indoor courts
    (c) Grass

17. Where is 'No man's land?'
    (a) That part of the court outside the baseline
    (b) That part of the court between the net and the service line
    (c) That part of the court between the baseline and service line

18. If you throw the ball up for a service and let it bounce instead of hitting it, where should it land, if thrown up correctly?
    (a) Just inside the baseline
    (b) On the baseline
    (c) Just outside the baseline

19. When lobbing, your racket head should finish in a much higher position than for the normal groundstrokes. If it doesn't, which of the following is the likely outcome?
    (a) You are likely to lean backwards as you hit the ball
    (b) The lob will land short in your opponent's court
    (c) Your opponent will have the opportunity to smash

20. To hit a lob with top spin which of the following grips is it advisable to adopt on the forehand?
    (a) Western
    (b) Semi-western
    (c) Continental

ANSWERS

21. If you want extra power in your strokes should you
    (a) increase the tension in the strings of your racket
    (b) reduce the tension in the strings

22. At what point does the ball reach its highest point with the flat forehand shot?
    (a) At impact
    (b) When going over the net
    (c) At a point level with your opponent's service line

ANSWERS

1. (a) Continental grip
2. (a) Slightly closed
3. (b) At a point between your knee and waist
4. (c) In line with it
5. (a) he has played a topspin forehand
6. (b) Six feet from the net
7. (c) On the baseline
8. (c) Next to each other, either on the baseline or up at the net
9. (b) Throw the ball up slightly in front of you and to the right of you
10. All are valid reasons but the best is: (a) Because it slows the shot down and gives your opponent more chance of recovery
11. (b) Lob, because it will force him into the back of the court

12. (a) To take the speed off the ball. The other two are also important, but they are important in all tennis strokes
13. (b) Make sure your non-racket arm is outstretched
14. (a) Head high
15. (a) Balls hit wide of him, and (b) Balls hit low
16. (c) Grass, because it is a fast surface
17. (c) That part of the court between the baseline and service line
18. (a) Just inside the baseline
19. All three . . .
20. (b) Semi-western
21. (a) Reduce the tension. It is a fallacy that a highly strung racket gives more power
22. (b) When going over the net.

Another of the rising stars, Michael Chang. He is seen here playing the baseline game on clay.

GLOSSARY

Alley: American colloquialism for the area between the tramlines.

American twist: A 'kick' service where the racket is taken towards the right hand side of the body, applying vicious side spin to the ball.

Backcourt: Area of court between the sidelines, the service line and the baseline.

Backhand: For the right-handed player, any stroke played from the left side of the body, usually with the back of the hand, the right foot and shoulder towards the net.

Backhand grip: The thumb straight up the racket, or diagonally across it.

Ball: Can be white or yellow, and must be $2\frac{1}{2}$–$2\frac{5}{8}$ in (6.35–6.7 cm) in diameter, and weight 2–$2\frac{1}{16}$ oz (56.7–58.7 g). If dropped from 100 in (254 cm) onto concrete it must bounce 53–58 in (135–147 cm).

Ball in play: A ball is in play from when it is struck at service to when the point is scored or a let called.

Baseline The line parallel to the net at each end of the court.

Centre mark: A line inside the court at its centre point, at right angles to the baseline, 4 in (10.16 cm) long, 2 in (5.08 cm) wide.

Changing ends: Players change ends after every odd numbered game. One minute is allowed for this procedure.

Chop: Striking the ball from top to bottom so that the underside spins upwards, towards the line of flight. This keeps the ball low and restricts the bounce.

Closed grip: The racket faces down from the vertical. Also called the western grip.

Continental grip: Like the eastern grip, except the palm is more on top of the handle. To form it, the right hand moves to the left until the thumb and index fingers form a V on the left hand bevel of the handle.

Court dimensions: The court is 78 ft (23.77 m) long. In singles it is 27 ft (18.23. m) wide. In doubles it is 36 ft (10.97 m) wide. It is divided by a net 3 ft 6 in (1.07 m) high at the sides and 3 ft (.91 m) at the centre. 21 ft (6.4 m) either side of and parallel to the net are the centre lines. (The first tennis courts were hourglass shaped, like a figure of eight).

Deuce: 40–40 score. Derived from 'two to play' in French.

Down the line: Stroke played parallel to and near the line.

Drive: A hard-hit forehand or backhand stroke, usually from the back of the court, using a flat faced racket or topspin.

Drop shot: A ball struck gently, with backspin, designed to catch out an opponent positioned well away from the net or shot direction.

Eastern grip: Palm parallel with the racket face, flat against the handle.

Fault: Called on a service if
 a) Both feet are not behind the baseline and on the correct side of the centre mark.
 b) Ball strikes ground before hitting the racket.

GLOSSARY

c) Ball hit twice.

d) Server materially changes position before delivery.

e) Ball does not reach diagonally opposing service court.

Forecourt: Area between sidelines, net and service line.

Formations: There are a number of doubles formations, involving switching positions or staying at the baseline or the net, depending on the game strategy.

Grand Slam: Winning the four major championships (Australian, French, Wimbledon and USA) in one year.

Groundstrokes: Shot made after the ball has bounced.

Let: If the linesman's decision is disputed or reversed, a point is replayed.

Line judge: Ten line judges plus the net cord and foot fault judge are required for championship matches.

Net cord: If the service hits the net and lands in the correct service court, the point is replayed.

Open grip: The racket face inclines up instead of vertically. Also called the 'continental' grip.

Order of service: The first server is chosen by whoever wins toss or the racket or a spun coin. In doubles, the order of service can be changed for each new set.

Percentage tennis: Strategy based on prioritising points which really need to be won. For example, increase your attack on the opponent's serve at 0–30.

Poaching: Intercepting in doubles play, to surprise opponents or protect partner.

Ranking: The international and national gradings of players.

Rough: The thin strings at the top and bottom of the racket present a rough surface on one side, smooth the other.

Rubber: Individual match in team competition such as the Davis Cup.

Service line: 21 ft (6.4 m) line either side of and parallel to the net. Marks the boundary of the service court.

Sideline: There are four sidelines on the court, all running its length to mark the outer boundary in singles and doubles play.

Slice: Ball struck with underspin and a glancing blow, taking the ball to one side with a long, flat bounce.

Slow-balling: Gentle, usually spinning returns to take the pace off the ball.

Sphairistike: Greek-derived name of early, popular form of lawn tennis patented by Major Walter Clopton Wingfield in (1873). Name soon shortened to 'Sticky' by the Victorians.

Tennis elbow: Pain in lower end of funny bone, or humerus, caused by inflammation of the tendon.

Tramlines: The pair of sidelines.

INDEX

Page references in **bold** refer to photographs.

INDEX

Also available in the Ward Lock
Ahead of the Game series:

GOLF by P.G.A. Captain Richard Bradbeer 07063 6884 3

SQUASH by England international and S.R.A. Coach David
Pearson 07063 6885 1

SOCCER by F.A. Coach Mike McGlynn 07063 6886 X